T H E
Affordable
H O R S E

Also by Sharon B. Smith

The Performance Mare: Maximizing What Your Mare Does Best

THE
Affordable
HORSE

A Guide to Low-Cost Ownership

SHARON B. SMITH

Howell Book House
New York

Maxwell Macmillan Canada
Toronto

Maxwell Macmillan International
New York Oxford Singapore Sydney

636.1
smI

Howell Book House
Macmillan Publishing Company
866 Third Avenue
New York, NY 10022

Maxwell Macmillan Canada, Inc.
1200 Eglinton Avenue East
Suite 200
Don Mills, Ontario M3C 3N1

Macmillan Publishing Company is part of the Maxwell Communication Group
of Companies.

All photographs by Sharon B. Smith unless otherwise noted.

Library of Congress Cataloging-in-Publication Data

Smith, Sharon B.
    The affordable horse : a guide to low-cost ownership / Sharon B. Smith.
        p.   cm.
    Includes index.
    ISBN 0-87605-966-3
    1. Horses—Costs.   2. Horses.   3. Horses—Buying.   I. Title.
SF285.33.S58   1994
    636.1—dc20   93-36774   CIP

BT 17.00/10.54 7/94

Macmillan books are available at special discounts for bulk purchases for sales
promotions, premiums, fund-raising, or educational use. For details, contact:

Special Sales Director
Macmillan Publishing Company
866 Third Avenue
New York, NY 10022

10 9 8 7 6 5 4 3 2 1

Printed in the United States of America

Book Design by Diane Stevenson / SNAP•HAUS GRAPHICS

C O N T E N T S

CONTENTS

INTRODUCTION

To many of us, the horse is a symbol of what is right with the world. In spite of generations of careful breeding, the horse still seems to be just a step or two out of the wild. In spite of training and confinement, the horse at gallop seems just a step or two from freedom. The horse conjures up images of a less stressful time, of the untamed frontier, of the healthful out-of-doors.

Besides, horseback riding is a sport that does not require years of practice to enjoy but still does provide nearly limitless opportunity to develop skill and subtlety. It's ironic that many people are discovering the special pleasures of horses just as access to them becomes more limited. There are fewer trail-ride stables, fewer lesson barns, fewer places where you can simply stop your car and watch horses graze.

Ownership is the answer. With your own horse, you can ride a horse you like and trust and you can do it when you want to. You can practice riding skills to your heart's content, not worrying about the clock that signals the end of a lesson. You can gaze on your horse for hours if you feel so inclined, not worrying about somebody else coming along to tack him up and ride him away.

But horse ownership is an unfulfilled dream for most people. They're convinced that only the rich can afford the considerable expense of buying and keeping horses. That fear is understandable. In the northeastern United States and in California, a young, well-trained horse, but not one of top show-quality can cost $5,000 or $6,000. Full board without special training runs $200 to $1,000 a month, shoeing might be $80 every six weeks, vet bills can average $100 a year for a healthy horse. Prices are somewhat lower in other parts of the country, but usually not much. It does indeed seem like a hobby for rich people.

But price is relative. A good horse will cost less than a good car, and his yearly maintenance and depreciation will be about the same. But the changing role of the horse means that most people don't consider the expenses to be comparable. Until the early part of this century, almost anybody who could afford the expense maintained at least one horse, with no more than an occasional grumble at the cost. Nowadays, with most horses used only for companionship and sport, it's not a question of grumbling. Most people simply refuse to spend the kind of money necessary to buy and board a horse. A car is a necessity; a horse is a luxury.

But most people give up too soon. It is possible for people of average income to own horses without going deeply into debt while doing it. Most of the essential expenses of horse ownership can be reduced dramatically, and it can be done without compromising the health and comfort of the horse.

I owned horses when I had the substantial income of a television anchorwoman, and I owned horses when I had the erratic—and never very large—income of a freelance writer. The horses never knew the difference. They were equally happy and performed equally well.

How about me? I certainly worked harder when I had to watch the bills. I spent time looking for bargains, I spent time reading and learning so I would know that my limited money was being well spent, and I spent plenty of time doing ordinary physical labor. But I certainly didn't enjoy horse ownership any less. In fact, the opposite was true.

Saving money in horse ownership will invariably mean extra work, but it doesn't have to be a heavy burden of time and commitment. You can save a little, or you can save a lot. The choice is up to you.

Acquiring Your Horse

The Giveaway Horse

As you begin to look for your affordable horse, you must understand one irrefutable fact of modern equine life and keep that fact in mind throughout your search. No matter how troubled the national economy, no matter how difficult tax laws make it for professional horse owners to turn a profit, and no matter what farm regulations do to the ability of livestock breeders to earn a living, almost no horse is worth nothing.

He can be old, hopelessly lame, and so hard to handle that he cannot be used, but he is still worth several hundred dollars to an owner determined to get some money out of him. He is always worth what horse people call "killer price." That is the amount of money a horse of his weight will bring from a dealer who buys animals for slaughter.

Several hundred thousand horses go through packing plants each year in North America, with some of their meat going to Europe for human consumption and the rest remaining here to go into pet food cans. Many good-natured and useful horses are included in that figure. Killer price reached 60 cents a pound on the hoof in my area recently, and that means the average-sized riding horse is worth $500 to $700 as meat. The price fluctuates according to demand, season, and region, but it's unlikely ever to drop below two or three hundred dollars again. At many—possibly most— horse auctions nowadays, any horse who sells for killer price or less is almost certainly on his way to a slaughterhouse.

Does that mean you're going to have to pay as much as $700 to get a horse of any kind these days, usable or not? Not at all. You can find a usable horse for nothing, although you will have to do some searching.

Many owners, even those in desperate financial straits, love their horses enough to be willing to give up money to assure a good life for animals they can no longer keep. Some of these people actively search out new homes for their horses. Other owners may not work quite so hard to find alternatives to the killers but will happily forego a few hundred dollars if an alternative presents itself to them. The secret to finding the truly affordable horse is to make contact with those people.

THE GIVEAWAY PLEASURE HORSE

The first group of horse owners to search out are those who own pleasure horses. Here's how to find them.

Classified Ads
Giveaway horses often appear in classified ads, but rarely do they show up in the pages of regular newspapers. They do

appear occasionally in the classified sections of national horse magazines, but giveaways are most likely to be found in regional horse publications. In fact, the smaller the region covered by the publication, the more likely it is to include regular giveaway ads. Not only are advertising rates lower in local horse publications, but owners probably feel that they will have a better chance of assuring the placement of their horses in good homes if the people who respond to the ad live nearby. In fact, I have on my desk the current issue of a horse newspaper that covers a few counties in southern Connecticut—an area of perhaps fifty miles square—and it includes ads for four giveaways.

You probably won't find regional horse publications in the racks of your neighborhood newsstand, unless you live in a

The classified sections of horse publications often carry ads for giveaway horses.

very horsey neighborhood. Instead, visit a tack shop or feed store. Even if they don't carry the publications, they will probably be able to tell you what's being published in your area, when it comes out, and where to find it.

Bulletin Boards

While you're at the tack or feed store, take a look at the bulletin board that's almost certainly there. The board is likely to be a gold mine of information on reasonably priced horses, boarding stables, equipment, and other items of interest. Giveaway ads are not quite so common, but they do show up now and then. Write down the numbers of any prospects, but take a few moments to put up a card of your own. Write something like "I can offer a good home to your unwanted horse," then add your name and telephone number at the bottom. It will be obvious that you're looking for a giveaway or a very low-priced horse, and nobody will call offering you a bargain $5,000 dressage prospect.

Word of Mouth

Some of the best-loved, most useful giveaway horses are not advertised anywhere, in spite of their owners' eagerness to find new homes for them. Dealers in horses for slaughter look for reasonably priced horses wherever they can find them, including classified ads. Some owners fear that advertising might put their horses into the hands of a dealer.

You could spend years hoping to hear talk of a prospect while waiting in line at the bank, so you must approach people more likely than you to hear about potential giveaways. That includes people who have contact with a lot of different horse owners. Visit or call boarding stable managers, tell them what you hope to find, and leave your name

Usable, well-loved giveaways can sometimes be found through word of mouth from farriers, vets, and other horse-care professionals.

and number in case they hear of people who can no longer keep their horses. Do the same with feed store employees and horseshoers. Each may have clients who are having trouble paying the bills. If they know of a possible giveaway, they will be happy to bring a potential new owner in contact with the old one and maintain a paying client.

Large animal veterinary offices may also offer prospects. Many maintain bulletin boards for you to check and post. Even if they don't, you may leave your name and number with the receptionist, the animal technician, or the vet. Don't expect them to institute a search for you, but they are likely to pass your name on to an owner who needs a new home for his horse. Like the feed store and the horseshoer, a vet would rather keep a client than see it sold to a broker. If you acquire a giveaway through a vet, you may even get a free health assessment of your new horse as part of the deal.

Problems of the Giveaway Pleasure Horse

There will almost certainly be a catch. Out there somewhere may be an exceedingly rich person who gives away a perfect specimen of horseflesh simply because she's tired of him, but don't count on it. Most free horses come with problems.

Few responsible owners would offer—and you shouldn't consider—a horse who is truly ill, with infectious disease, active founder, or anything else that causes serious pain and requires ongoing medical treatment. It's usually a lesser problem that you have to worry about with the free horse.

The owner may well tell you about the problem up front. Since he's not looking to make money on the deal, he may be more likely to be honest than somebody trying to sell a horse. You may discover the problem in your own examination of the horse, or you may learn about it if you decide to have the horse vetted. See Chapter 2 for thoughts about paying for a veterinary examination of a free or low-priced horse. Any chronic illness or lameness can turn a horse into a giveaway; most giveaways will have one of the following specific problems discussed below.

Age

The simple fact of advancing age is most likely to cause a horse to become a giveaway, but extra years may or may not make him less useful. Whether age should be considered a problem depends on the condition of the horse and the use you intend to make of him.

Experts usually set the average life expectancy of a horse at twenty years. That's probably accurate, if the average includes all horses and all causes of death, including foal mortality and injury-caused deaths of young performing horses. A twenty-year-old horse is rarely elderly, although he may be somewhat more subject to illness and injury than a younger horse.

I have owned, adopted, shared, and cared for several older horses, and I now believe that most well-treated horses don't begin to even look elderly until at least the age of twenty-five. Many still remain useful for light work well after they start to show their age, when the muzzle begins to go gray and the back starts to dip.

As to how much and how hard they can be used, that depends on the individual. Most owners would not expect constant, strenuous work from a horse in his later years, but others do with no apparent harm to the horse. The famous nineteenth-century trotting mare Goldsmith Maid set the last of her many world records for the mile in 1876 at the age of nineteen. This century, several Grand Prix jumpers continued at the highest levels of international competition into their late teens. A healthy horse in his late teens or early twenties is fully capable of normal pleasure use and should not be rejected for age alone.

Navicular Disease

Horses with chronic lameness problems are next most likely—after aged horses—to show up in the giveaway ranks. A substantial percentage of these suffer from navicular disease, a chronic and incurable foot condition that makes a horse incapable of doing work that causes repeated concussion to the feet. Many of these horses are relatively young, often under the age of twelve. Some navicular horses can gallop and jump a little, while others cannot even canter. Many horses with navicular disease can do normal walk-trot work in a ring or on a trail without discomfort.

Navicular disease is caused by inflammation of the area surrounding the navicular bone or destruction of the bone itself. It is usually brought on by heavy work on hard surfaces. Big horses with small feet and straight pasterns are particularly vulnerable. You often find jumpers and western performance horses among navicular sufferers.

While it's best not to acquire a horse with navicular disease if you can help it, many victims can live long, useful lives with proper shoeing, careful handling, and occasional veterinary care. If you are offered a navicular horse, ask to speak to the vet and farrier who've cared for him. If necessary, request that the owner make the contact for you. When asked about an unsound giveaway horse, most professionals will be honest about what you can expect from him.

Heaves

Another chronic, incurable condition that shows up in giveaway horses is the respiratory disease called heaves, also known as broken wind. Like navicular disease, heaves is common, sometimes progressive, limiting, but not necessarily devastating to the horse's useful future. Unlike navicular, it appears most often in older horses.

Heaves usually develops after a horse recovers from an upper respiratory infection, sometimes long after the infection has been cured. The first sign may be a chronic cough.

Other symptoms include a progressive lack of endurance and shortness of breath. You can spot a horse with advanced heaves by a characteristic double pump of the flanks when the horse breathes out. That sign can't be masked.

Damage to the lungs caused by the initial infection has made the horse vulnerable to irritants and allergens, and that's what makes his breathing labored. Severe cases can be so debilitating that the horse must be destroyed, but they are rare. More common are cases that can be managed, often without medication.

A horse with heaves can usually be used for moderate, regular work if his environment can be kept reasonably free of irritants, including stall and hay dust. A vet or a good horse health book (see Chapter 9 for suggestions) will give you advice on maintaining a horse with heaves. Be sure to look at a recent book, since new and promising methods of heaves treatment have appeared in the last few years.

A minor case of heaves should not disqualify a horse from consideration, unless your idea of horse ownership includes several hours a day of fast, hard use. The disease will mean more work for you, and you should read extensively on what might be required to control your horse's case before committing yourself to ownership.

One more warning. Remember that heaves often gets worse as a horse ages, in spite of the best of care. A horse sufficiently healthy for your purposes now may not be so useful a few years down the line.

RACEHORSE CASTOFFS

The three most common problems that appear in pleasure horse giveaways—advanced age, navicular disease, and heaves—rarely show up in prospects from another huge pool of potential free horses—racetrack rejects. Nobody is sure exactly how many North American Thoroughbred and Standardbred racehorses reach the end of their racing careers each year, but the figure could be as high as 25,000, since as many as 40,000 new foals of the two breeds are born each spring. Those who no longer win enough money to pay their training expenses become "castoffs."

A few retirees have the pedigrees and race records to become breeding stock. Of the others, some have good enough conformation—as well as an owner or trainer willing to find a buyer—to be resold as hunter, jumper, or saddle horse prospects. A lucky but minuscule minority become pets of their owners.

Thousands simply disappear from the track, sold cheaply or given away to dealers who haul them to auctions or directly to slaughterhouses. These horses are old only by racetrack standards, where six is old, seven is elderly, and eight is positively ancient. Many are lame only by racetrack standards, where "racing sound" is something entirely different from normal equine soundness. Some are difficult to handle, but no more so than any horse who has been taught nothing more than to tolerate a rider and carry him in the general direction he requests.

Many owners and trainers feel guilty about what happens to their castoffs, but they also feel there's nothing they can afford to do with a horse who no longer earns his living. There is, but most owners won't go looking for it.

Locating the Castoff

There are a few organizations that take unwanted former racehorses and place them in adoptive homes. The organiza-

As many as 25,000 Thoroughbreds retire from the racetrack each year. Most are still sound enough for any equine activity except racing.

tions are small, usually underfunded, and rely mostly on the energy and kind hearts of the people who run them. They also tend to come and go. Here's one that has stayed:

California Equine Retirement Foundation
34033 Kooden Road
Winchester, CA 95366
(714) 926-4190

This organization has placed dozens of castoff racehorses with new owners. It provides a permanent home for many other unadoptable ones.

To find a racehorse adoption organization closer to your area, call the publicity office of a nearby racetrack. Somebody in the office is likely to know if there's a functioning organization to place racetrack rejects from that track.

Even if you do locate an organization, you may discover that it's so underfunded and so understaffed that there are few horses available for adoption. In that case, you will have to conduct the search yourself. You must go right to the source.

It's not easy for an outsider to get into a racetrack barn area. At every parimutuel racetrack in the country, a security guard is supposed to check credentials, licenses, or passes before allowing anybody in. In reality, strangers do get in, especially at smaller tracks. But it will be more efficient for you to make contact with someone who knows what's going on rather than wander around a barn area asking about unwanted horses. There are several good places to make your interest known.

The HBPA

Nearly every Thoroughbred track has a branch office or a representative of the Horsemen's Benevolent and Protective Association or a similar group that functions as a trainers' union. Although the local offices vary dramatically in the level of contact they maintain with trainers, most offices offer a good opportunity to make your willingness to adopt a castoff known to a number of trainers. Some publish newsletters and might include your offer in their next one. Some maintain bulletin boards. Even if the receptionist or office manager can't think of any way of publicizing your request, ask him or her to take your name and telephone number. They may hear of something and pass the information on to you. Everybody involved in horse racing would rather see a castoff go to a pleasure home than to the slaughterhouse. To find a local HBPA branch, you can contact the national headquarters:

> *Horsemen's Benevolent and Protective Association*
> *2800 Grand Route*
> *Saint John Street*
> *New Orleans, LA 70119*
> *(504) 945-4500*

You can also ask the publicity office of a local racetrack for the number of their local HBPA or similar organization.

The Standardbred racing industry has no exact equivalent of the HBPA, but most tracks have a relationship with some group that provides many of the same functions. Call the publicity office for information on their trainers' group. In fact, since harness tracks tend to be more informal and accessible than many Thoroughbred tracks, feel free to tell the publicity people exactly what you're looking for. Tell them that you're willing to adopt a castoff and they might do some of the legwork for you.

Track Officials

Racetrack officials, primarily those who deal with the trainers rather than the public, often know of horses about to be cast off. Every track has a Racing Secretary (although he's sometimes known as the Director of Racing), whose job it is to supply horses for races. He does this by scheduling races and allocating purses suitable for the kind of horses handled by local trainers. He's also ultimately responsible for assigning stall space, which is supplied free at most racetracks, to horses most likely to run and provide sport for fans and bettors.

The Racing Secretary is an important figure at every racetrack and almost always knows more than anyone else about what's going on with individual trainers and horses. At large, wealthy tracks he's also an important executive. At those tracks, you may find you have better access to a lesser official, who usually goes by the title of Stall Supervisor. Call the track and ask for the name and office telephone number of either or both of these officials. When you call their offices, identify yourself as a person willing to adopt a castoff and ask to leave your name and number. They may be able to put you in contact with the trainer of a horse who is young, sound, but just too slow to race successfully, or one who's not racing sound but still usable. The track officials will be as happy as the trainer to get an unraceable horse out of the barn area and open his stall to a better horse.

Racetrack Veterinarians

Track vets may help you locate racehorses with injuries, if you're unable to find a sound one. With any luck, they will also tell you about the limitations of those injuries. Track vets, like track officials, are busy and are unlikely to institute a major search for you. But they do hear about unraceable horses on a regular basis and may give you the name of a trainer who has one. There are two kinds of track vets. One, usually called the state vet, works for the racetrack. His or her job is to check a horse for soundness on race day, to be present for on-track emergencies, or to supervise pre- and post-race drug testing. State vets hear about potential cast-offs, but not so often as does the second kind of track vet.

Private practitioners who are licensed to operate in the barn areas of racetracks have individual, professional relationships with trainers and often know about potential adoptees. They are tricky for the outsider to find, since many never list their practices in the Yellow Pages and some don't even have offices. Racetrack receptionists, the local HBPA, and even the publicity office can usually tell you how to get a message to one. Again, the message is the same. Say you are looking for a castoff and leave your name and telephone number.

Problems of the Racetrack Castoff

Most horses fail as racehorses because they're just too slow to win enough money to pay for the cost of upkeep and training. Slow is relative, of course. The slowest racing-bred Thoroughbred will be faster than almost any other horse you are likely to find. If your potential adoptee is slow but sound, his lack of speed should be welcomed. But he may be slow because of injury, and you should assess the implications of the injury before you commit to ownership.

Racetrack Injury

Some former racehorses are hopelessly crippled and will never take a sound step again in their lives. Trainers generally don't try to unload these as giveaways, although they may. More likely, you will be offered a horse with a serious leg problem that should improve with rest that the trainer and owner can't afford, considering the talent level of the horse. Soft tissue injuries are common, including bowed tendons and curbs. Bone problems like splints and ringbone can also make a horse temporarily lame.

Many of these injuries improve with a few months of rest, although the horse may never be sound enough for serious jumping, hunting, eventing, or other extremely strenuous activities. He will be sound enough for pleasure use, even heavy use. Trainers and track vets are reasonably likely to give an honest assessment of a giveaway. Listen to them, then make your own decision about the potential of the individual horse.

If you adopt a horse from a Standardbred track, you will have another problem—possibly two. Most racing Standardbreds have never carried riders, so they will have to be broken to ride. But Standardbreds tend to be extremely calm and good natured and those who have raced have spent their lives being touched, handled, harnessed, and used, so it's rarely difficult to teach a former harness racer to carry a rider. But it's not so easy to teach a pacer to trot.

The majority of Standardbreds in North America today are pacers, and you are much more likely to be offered a pacer than a trotter as a castoff. Some are actually natural trotters and will invariably trot when they are not wearing their harness hopples. Others prefer to pace, and switching these to the trot may be a challenge. Toe weights on shoes often help, and a farrier who has worked with Standardbreds will be worth his weight in gold during the retraining process. On the whole, Standardbreds retire from the racetrack sounder than Thoroughbreds, and don't let the fact that a prospect paces and pulls a sulky turn you off. Neither is a real problem.

Most horses of either breed come off the racetrack poorly broken in comparison to horses raised for pleasure use. Some are very difficult to handle. But once they settle into a more normal horse life, complete with turnout, affectionate handling, and individual attention, most adjust happily to careers as pleasure horses. Some remain difficult forever, but remember that some horses who've never been near a racetrack are difficult as well.

RESCUED HORSES

Not only racehorses require rescue from uncertain fates. Particularly during difficult economic times, horses of all breeds end up in the custody of animal welfare organizations. Many become available for adoption.

Equine Organizations

There are a handful of organizations across the country that specialize in horse rescue and placement. Like their counterparts within the Thoroughbred business, they sometimes come and go as a result of the difficulty in raising money and finding help. Here is an outstanding example that has managed to survive for several years:

Colorado Horse Rescue
P.O. Box 1510
Arvada, CO 80001-1510
(303) 469-5863

Rescue services closer to your home may be located by contacting one of the following national humane organizations, each of which may be able to direct you to an equine rescue group in your region.

American Horse Protection Association
1000 29th Street N.W.
Suite T-100
Washington, DC 20007
(202) 965-0500

American Society for the Prevention
of Cruelty to Animals
424 East 92nd Street
New York, NY 10128
(212) 876-7700

Hooved Animal Humane Society
P.O. Box 400
Woodstock, IL 60098
(815) 337-5563

Humane Society of the United States
2100 L Street N.W.
Washington, DC 20037
(202) 452-1100

THE GIVEAWAY HORSE

Animal Shelters

Areas that lack rescue organizations specific to horses aren't exempt from horses that need help. In these areas, local officials who find abused or abandoned horses are likely to contact a local or state SPCA office. In most cases, these organizations handle only small animals, but many maintain lists of people willing to take in horses.

Call your local animal shelter and ask that they keep your name on file should they be faced with placing a horse, and ask them for the telephone number of the state SPCA, which is more likely to have horses available at any given time.

Shelters, both general and horse-specific, often charge adoption fees to people taking their animals. Don't begrudge the money. In exchange for the fee, you will get an honest assessment of the horse's health and prospects. You may also get a horse who has already been given a year's worth of vaccinations as well as a period of decent feed and treatment. You may even get free delivery. Besides, the money couldn't possibly go to a better cause.

WILD HORSE ADOPTION

The U.S. Department of the Interior's Bureau of Land Management has run a wild-horse adoption program for more than twenty years. The program was designed to remove wild horses and burros threatened with starvation from over-grazed land and place them in private homes.

The adoption program has been controversial, with opponents arguing that the placed horses represent just a drop in the bucket of those needing help and that some of those placed have been acquired by dealers who have sent them on to slaughterhouses. Nevertheless, thousands of threatened animals have found good homes and the program continues. The $125 adoption fee does not include transportation, but it does include vaccinations, worming, and a physical examination that proves the adoptee to be free of serious disease or injury.

It's a complicated program, involving twelve different centers, mostly in the western United States. For information on the program, as well as the address and telephone number of the center that serves your region, contact the headquarters of the program:

Adopt-A-Horse
Bureau of Land Management
U.S. Department of the Interior
Washington, DC 20240
(202) 653-9215

For more in-depth information and advice on wild horse adoption, pick up a copy of Barbara Eustis-Cross and Nancy Bowker's *The Wild Horse: An Adopter's Manual* (Howell Book House, 1992).

But remember that wild horses, particularly adult animals, are usually the most difficult of all giveaways to turn into usable pleasure horses. Unless you are experienced with horses—or willing to work out an arrangement with somebody who is—you should make every effort to find a giveaway from another source first.

C H A P T E R

T W O

The Low-Priced Horse

If you're willing to pay something for your horse, you will be able to choose from a larger, younger, and healthier group of animals than if you limit your search to giveaways. But you may have to be more careful of owners who try to conceal problems. Unlike the owners of giveaways, sellers have something to gain by trying to convince you to take their horses.

Most sellers are honest, but you can't tell the honest from the dishonest just by looking. Moreover, even an honest seller—one who would not try to mask problems—might not volunteer information about the same problems if they aren't visible and you fail to ask. To be fair, the dishonest seller of the horse with hidden problems appears at all levels of the price scale and there's an argument to be made for the idea that the more he has to gain from selling his horse, the harder a crooked seller will work to cheat.

Realistically, you can be reasonably assured that the low-priced horse will have some problems that have reduced his value. Your job is to identify those problems and decide whether they limit the horse's usefulness for your purposes. Keep in mind that phrase "for your purposes." A horse not healthy enough to steeplechase may be entirely healthy enough for any other reasonable use.

This chapter is not intended to tell you how to buy a good horse but rather to help you get the lowest price for the most usable horse you can find. Your best source of advice on overall horse buying is an experienced horse person whose judgment you trust. There are also books that offer valuable information. Here are three useful ones that contain detailed, well-illustrated chapters on picking out a good horse:

The Complete Book of Horse Care by Tim Hawcroft (Howell Book House, 1991)

Practical Horseman's Book of Horsekeeping by M. A. Stoneridge, ed. (Doubleday, 1983)

Understanding Your Horse's Health by Janet Eley (Ward Lock Ltd., 1992)

You will also find excellent horse-buying tips in books that focus on a particular horse sport. Identify the general use you anticipate for your horse, then take a look at a book in that category. For example, if you expect to do a little trail riding, you'll find the ideal trail horse described in a book on endurance riding. Just remember that you probably won't be able to find anything that approaches ideal in the low-priced category. But you may be able to avoid a purchase with a conformation flaw or a soundness problem that makes a horse totally unsuitable for your intended use.

WHAT DOES "LOW-PRICED" MEAN?

What's "low-priced" depends on the region, the economy, the intended use, the breed, and the individual horse. At the summer Thoroughbred yearling sales in Kentucky, a $30,000 yearling is cheap—probably a bitter disappointment and a financial blow to his breeder. He's certainly not cheap to you or me. You need to know what's going on in the horse market in your area before you can reasonably assess the problems of a potential purchase in relation to his price.

Generally speaking, anything below your region's killer price should be considered a giveaway with a pricetag. The owner could get more by selling the horse to a slaughter-house dealer. Don't expect a dealer—or any owner who lacks an emotional attachment to the horse—to do much negotiating for an animal being offered for killer price or less, which will probably be $250 to $600.

Above killer price, negotiating becomes possible. But how much you can expect to negotiate downward depends on the horse and the circumstances. You can determine a price range for a horse of a particular breed, age, and level of training by examining ads in local horse publications. You must know the price range, not only so you can save yourself embarrassment by spending time with the owner of a horse you'll never negotiate into an affordable range, but also so you can be realistic about the inevitable problems in a horse being offered for far below his apparent market value.

For example, in my region, if I see an average-sized warm-blood under the age of fourteen being offered for less than

$2,000, I can be pretty well assured that there is a serious problem with that horse. But I can find an average-sized Arabian of similar age for far less than that amount and stand a reasonable chance of getting a healthy, sound horse. In another region, the opposite may be true.

If you don't mind being considered nosy, ask friends and acquaintances what they paid for their horses. Most of them will tell you and offer some advice on what you can expect to find for a similar price.

After gathering information from horse owners and want ads, you must decide what "low-priced" means to you. My own feeling is that a low-priced horse is one that you buy for substantially less than what you would pay for a good individual but not major ribbon-winning member of his breed. That means $2,000 or less for a pleasure horse (maybe $1,000 or less during economic hard times).

PROBLEMS OF THE LOW-PRICED HORSE

Some horses are sold cheaply for the same reasons that others are given away, because they have problems that reduce their value in the open market. Giveaways and very low-priced horses tend to have many problems in common. Review Chapter 1 for thoughts on some of the reasons—including age and certain health limitations—that cause any horse's value to plummet.

Additional problems can reduce the value of a horse, although not quite so drastically. Here are some that you are likely to come across in your search for an affordable horse.

Vision Problems
Total blindness will almost always render a horse completely unusable, but blindness in one eye often has little effect,

except on his pricetag. The nature of the equine eye, which projects a fraction of an inch on the front side of his head, makes him both vulnerable to eye injury and able to cope quite well if he loses the sight in one of his eyes.

Although nearly every horse sport can offer an example of a one-eyed horse who's performed at the highest levels of competition, many show classes prohibit entry to horses with vision impairment. Hunter classes, most pleasure classes, and non-breeding stock halter classes are usually off-limits to the horse with a blind eye.

But horses with one eye see well enough for almost any sporting use. They lose a little of their ability to judge distances, but many learn to jump, run a barrel pattern, or perform nearly every other event with no apparent problems. Handlers do have to take a little extra care to talk to the horse when approaching from the blind side, but it's rarely a problem with an otherwise well-behaved animal. Handlers also have to be extra careful that the good eye isn't injured and be particularly vigilant about protruding hooks, nails, and other threats in stall and paddock.

The cosmetic effects as well as the prohibition from some show classes can cut the price of a partially blind horse in half or more, while reducing his usefulness by just a tiny percentage. Don't reject a good horse because of a vision impairment. Try him, both under saddle and on the ground, to see if he travels straight and doesn't stumble. Decide if he can do what you want. If he is a sensible horse, he probably can.

The Wrong-Sized Horse

A horse who's a few inches too short or too tall for his breed can be a great bargain. A horse bred to be a hunter or jumper has to be tall to be valuable, because that's what modern

The loss of her right eye made this Quarter Horse worth a fraction of her former value while reducing her usefulness hardly at all.

riders think they want. A 15-hand Holsteiner is not going to be worth anywhere near what a 16.2 member of his breed will be, no matter how good his conformation. A non-racing Thoroughbred increases in value for every inch he exceeds 15 hands.

Do you need a horse over 15 hands? If you are a woman interested in pleasure riding, almost certainly not. If you are a man, you might have to go to 15.2, but even you probably don't need anything much taller, unless you are especially tall yourself. You may have to find a muscular, heavy-framed horse, though, if you are heavy yourself. As soon as you convince yourself that you will be happy with a horse less than 16 hands, you will impressively increase your chances of finding a good, affordable horse.

Conversely, some ponies are too tall to qualify as ponies for competitive purposes, yet remain members of their pony breed and won't be thought of as horses. A pony who grows taller than 14.2 hands won't be permitted in pony classes and will probably look too big to parents buying a mount for their children. He will be the same well-bred, useful animal he would have been if he had stopped growing at 14.2 but will be worth far less than his slightly smaller full brother. At a little over 14.2, he will be big enough for many people. After all, Indian ponies and cow ponies of less than 15 hands carried adult men across the western plains.

Adults, particularly women, should make it a point to look at slightly overgrown ponies in their search for a low-priced prospect. You will often find these horses advertised as 14.2 hands (which they will be only if their owner trims their feet, doesn't shoe them, and puts a 200-pound weight on their back as they're measured).

Although a taller horse might look better, even a large man can be carried comfortably by a sturdy sub-15-hand horse.

THE LOW-PRICED HORSE

The Horse with a Vice

Some sound, healthy horses who show plenty of athletic ability still end up with bargain-basement pricetags because of behavior or unacceptable habits that their owners are unable to deal with. A single vice can turn a high-priced horse into an affordable one.

You will have two steps to take before making the decision to buy a horse with a vice. First, you have to be sure you know the vice you're facing. Second, you have to be sure you can either change the behavior or learn to live with it.

Here are a few ways to discover behavior problems in a potential purchase. The most important thing you can do is to handle him repeatedly, first on the ground and then in the saddle.

The ground handling should include these steps. If possible, bring the horse in from his field yourself. Tack him up before trying him. After riding, do a quick grooming, including picking up his feet. If his owner seems reluctant for you to do any of these things, expect to find a handling problem.

The horse may be annoyed at any of these steps without having a vice. But his annoyance should be nothing more than a second or two of pinned ears. A kick or bite is more serious. A refusal is equally serious, because you don't want to acquire a horse who needs a general anesthetic to be shod or vetted.

In the saddle, try him in conditions that approximate the circumstances in which you plan to use him. If he's going to have to go on a road to get to your trail rides, ask to try him near a moving car, although you may not want to actually try him in serious traffic. Have somebody clap hands, toss a crumpled-up piece of paper in front of him, or do anything else (within reason) that might cause a too-flighty horse to shy. Make sure your test is long enough so you can find out if your prospect is a puller, bucker, roller, or stumbler.

Stable vices are often harder to uncover, but getting a look at his stall might tell you if he's a stall-kicker, a cribber, or a horse who likes to play football with his feed bucket. Of course, you may not be able to watch long enough to discover a stall problem. Sometimes an owner can be encouraged to confess to hidden vices if you say you want a bill of sale that specifies the purchase to be free of known serious vices.

To decide whether or not you are willing or able to deal with the vice once you own the horse, you must assess your level of horsemanship and the seriousness of the vice. Here are two good books that include valuable information on how to handle horses with vices of various kinds:

The Horse's Mind by Lucy Rees (Prentice Hall, 1985)

The Problem Horse: An Owner's Guide by Karen Bush (Howell Book House, 1992)

As you'll learn in these books, as you will from experienced horse people, some vices are much easier to overcome than others. Stable vices tend to be easiest of all to handle. If you can provide plenty of turnout, you may never have to worry again about the most determined cribber or stall-kicker. Even under-saddle vices often disappear if the horse can spend several hours a day outside grazing and playing. Much bucking and bolting grow out of an excess of energy caused by too much standing around in a stall.

Other vices are much more difficult, and only extremely

experienced horse people should undertake ownership of horses with vices that endanger rider and handler. Even experienced riders should be careful. If you have any feeling whatsoever that a horse is actually trying to injure you, avoid him. No amount of money you're likely to save will be worth the chance you may be taking with your life and safety.

Some vices may require an investment in equipment to cure or to tolerate, but a little extra money may be a small price to pay if it means you can have a good horse for a price well below his value. You can buy a lot of $4.50 rubber feed tubs for the savings you might enjoy on a horse who destroys one every few weeks. A puller might be cured with a $15 rubber covered bit or a $20 dropped noseband cavesson.

The Unbroken or Green Horse

Leaving aside well-bred members of racing breeds, horses are worth less the younger they are, up to the point at which they are fully trained. With racehorses, hope and potential count for as much as performance, and most horses are worth more as unbroken yearlings than they will ever be again in their lives. Not so with virtually every other breed.

If you take a group of similarly bred, similarly conformed horses, the weanling will be cheapest, followed by the yearling, then the two-year-old who does a little ground work, then the three-year-old. After that, the horse begins to show talent or lack of it and his price fluctuates accordingly.

Unbroken horses, and those less than fully trained, sell for less because their owners know they face months or years of feed, vet, and shoeing bills before their animals can be used for their intended purposes. One of these horses can prove a great bargain to you in certain circumstances.

The first requirement is that you have access to reasonably

priced housing for the horse during its period of training. Check out Part Two for ideas. Some low-cost ways to house a trained horse (including its use in lesson programs) are unsuitable for the young horse in training, and you won't be able to consider them. Others, like full-time pasture boarding, are possible but hardly ideal, since a young horse needs more handling than it's likely to get when it's turned out twenty-four hours a day. That leaves backyard keeping, working for board, and other arrangements. If you can't work out a method to keep your untrained horse reasonably, you will use up any money saved by his low purchase price long before he's ready to work.

The second requirement that you should meet before taking on an untrained or green horse is the ability to handle the training. Experience in riding and grooming already-trained horses doesn't qualify you to train a young one. If you can't handle the training, you may find yourself having to hire a professional trainer. That will take the horse out of the affordable category too.

Here's an idea for the less experienced horse person who finds a bargain-priced young horse. Try to work out a shared ownership arrangement with somebody capable of doing the training. You supply the horse; he or she supplies the training. This kind of sharing is potentially beneficial to both parties, but it has the same pitfalls and advantages of other horse sharing. Check Chapter 3 for tips on this.

The Horse Out of Season
Often, just waiting a few months can make a horse affordable. Horse prices at all levels of quality tend to be highest in late spring and early summer, when people are thinking about riding and when good grazing makes for easier feeding

and care. Prices tend to sink in fall, as children return to school and as winter looms, prompting owners to realize they face the prospect of boarding a horse that's rarely ridden.

Sometimes you will notice a slight price jump in December as Christmas approaches. In many areas, a horse will be offered at its lowest possible price at the beginning of January.

WHERE TO FIND THE AFFORDABLE HORSE

Use the same sources you utilize in the search for the giveaway—horse publication classified ads, notices at stables, feed and tack stores, vet offices, and racetracks, and word of mouth. Check Chapter 1 for the procedure. When you put up notices yourself, or ask about prospects, emphasize the phrase "reasonably priced." Even though people have different ideas about what constitutes "reasonable," the phrase will let owners know that you're willing to pay something but that you're not looking for a five-figure show animal.

There is one additional source of low-priced horses, but it's one that requires caution. Auction houses around the country run horse sales on a regular basis. You'll find them advertised in local horse publications. There are good buys to be had, particularly at breeding stock sales that concentrate on a particular breed. Here you may find reasonably healthy horses that fit into one of the affordable categories, including unbroken weanlings or yearlings with a conformation flaw that might prevent their use in their intended sport but not in other sports. You are likely to find older, barren mares who are still young enough to be ridden for years. You may also find hopelessly unsound animals.

The racetrack is a good source of sound, high-quality, low-priced horses whose only problem is lack of racing speed.

General auction houses vary in quality, in terms of their willingness for you to test and check the horses ahead of time and their return policies. Buying an affordable auction horse is a risky business at best. Even if you figure that you can return an unsuitable one to the next auction, count on paying a consignment fee as well as probably not getting back what you put into buying and trailering. It's an alternative, but you must be extra cautious in your pre-purchase checking and testing.

THE PRE-PURCHASE VET EXAM

The formal vet exam is something that is almost always done in the case of an expensive horse but often skipped for a cheaper one. Whether you want to invest in a vet check depends on its cost, the cost of the horse, and what you can do with the horse if he turns out to be unusable. It also depends on your confidence in your own ability to spot illnesses and lameness in a horse you don't know.

Vets vary in their approaches to a pre-purchase exam. Call around to find out what the ones in your area do. Some have a set fee for such an exam, and they insist on particular tests. The fee can range from $100 to $200, depending on the vet's policies and depending on whether the vet comes to the horse or the horse goes to the vet. This fee generally doesn't include X-rays of feet and legs, which will cost at least $40 per limb.

Other vets will charge according to how much or how little you want. On average, expect to pay $20 to $25 for the basic clinic visit (if you have a trailer to get the horse there) or $30 to $35 if you need the vet to visit the farm. On top of that, a basic health examination will cost $30 to $40. Blood work should be $20 without a Coggins test for equine anemia, $40 with one.

There are two ways to approach the vet exam. One is to pay nothing for the horse until the exam is done, not even a deposit. The other is to contract for the horse, pay a deposit, with the balance due upon successful completion of the exam. Either way will cost you money if the horse fails.

The vet should be hired by you, not the owner, and you should be there during the examination. Particularly with low-priced horses, it's difficult for a vet to tell you whether or not you should buy a particular horse. Instead, you are likely to hear about the pros and cons of a given condition. The exam is useful beyond its value in making a decision about purchase. Take advantage of the visit to get advice on care and maintenance of the particular horse.

If you do go ahead with the purchase, have the vet administer any necessary vaccines at that time. The vaccines are cheaper than the visit, so you can save the cost of an additional vet trip by having them done immediately.

C H A P T E R

T H R E E

Horse Sharing

An arrangement that allows you to cut in half the cost of horse acquisition and maintenance might be just what you need to make ownership affordable for you. Sharing a horse may be the answer to your dreams, saving you time, money, and worry. Or it might prove to be a nightmare, leaving you with most of the costs and little of the pleasure of ownership. The key to a successful sharing arrangement is choosing the right partner, then being scrupulous about fairness—both your own and that of your sharing partner.

PICKING A PARTNER

Ironically, the person you are most likely to choose as a horse-sharing partner may prove to be least suitable in some important characteristics. Friends who share your time and interests are certainly easier to locate than strangers. But whether you pick a friend or choose a potential partner from another source, such as people who answer your ad on a stable bulletin board or those referred to you by a barn manager, subject every candidate to the same scrutiny. You may find that a friend, as much as you like and trust her, doesn't qualify in at least one very important way. Here are the important qualities to look for in a sharing partner.

Different Schedule

Remember that there will be only one horse between two people. If you and your prospective partner have the same work or school schedule, there will almost certainly be resentment or even conflict over riding time and barn work. The best partnerships are those between people with different days off and different working hours. If you work Monday through Friday, nine to five, try your best to find a partner whose days off fall on weekdays or who works nights. This way, one of you will be available for morning horse care and riding and the other for the afternoon chores and use. One can have all-day use on two weekdays, the other on the weekend days.

Close friends are often least likely to have differing schedules, since the friendship probably grew out of work, school, or being somewhere at the same time. Moreover, you won't be able to ride with your friend unless one of you rents or borrows a second horse. Conflict is almost guaranteed.

If you are determined to own a horse in partnership with someone in spite of similar schedules, take extra care to make rules for riding and barn work. Do it before problems develop.

Trustworthiness

You must be able to trust your partner to live up to the arrangements you work out for use, work, and expenses. Obviously it's easier to assess a friend or acquaintance than a stranger. Be honest with yourself in your assessment. Your prospective partner may be a good friend whose lack of promptness you've always overlooked. You may think it's amusing that her apartment is a mess, and that her telephone is sometimes turned off because she forgets to pay the bill. Her behavior won't be amusing in a partner in horse ownership.

Look for promptness in arriving at scheduled meetings, willingness to do the groundwork in looking for horses or boarding arrangements, and other signs that your partner is serious. If you ride at a lesson or rental stable with your partner, see if she is willing to tack and untack herself, and to groom her horse before and after the ride. If she's not, don't count on her doing much of the boring and tiring aspects of horse care.

If your prospective partner is a stranger, you should pay particular attention to his attitude during the search for the horse or the working out of the boarding arrangement— both his promptness at following through on what he has promised to do and his willingness to do his share of the planning and searching.

You may also ask for references from somebody you don't know well. The would-be partner may be the friend of a friend, or you may have mutual acquaintances. He may have taken riding lessons from an instructor you can call. Ask anybody who knows him, "I'm thinking of sharing the ownership of a horse with so-and-so. Do you think it will work out?"

THE AFFORDABLE HORSE

Ability to Pay

As you will see in subsequent chapters, you can keep a horse very cheaply. But you usually can't do it for no cost whatsoever, and you should try to find out if your partner is really willing and able to pay his share. Otherwise, you may lose most of the benefits of sharing because you will find yourself paying most of the bills.

The process of horse and board hunting will usually give you an idea of the financial capabilities of a potential partner. A person who won't pay for a long-distance telephone call to check on a promising giveaway, winces at the prospect of sharing a $75 a month pasture board bill, or argues that a horse doesn't need an $8 influenza shot before you take him home probably can't afford even affordable horsekeeping.

Similar Goals

You will be happiest and most comfortable with a person whose goals in horse ownership are similar to your own. If you want to trail ride each weekend and she dreams of competing in horse shows, you will have conflicts. You will probably have to turn down prospects suitable to you but not her, you may have to pay for a level of care necessary for a show horse but not a riding horse, and you may find yourself sharing the cost of corrective shoeing that a trail horse doesn't need. You may also find yourself unable to use the horse on your only free days.

Knowledge and Skill

You are almost always better off sharing a horse with someone who has knowledge and skill in horse care, preferably more knowledge than you do yourself. If your partner knows nothing, you will inevitably do more of the work. That may be acceptable to you, if the partner is suitable in every other way. Just don't get into an arrangement with somebody so incapable that they don't do any of the money-saving work while paying only half the expenses. As you'll see next, you can work out arrangements where the harder-working partner pays a lower percentage of the unavoidable costs.

WORKING OUT THE ARRANGEMENT

The word to remember in working out a partnership arrangement is "fair." The division of labor must be fair, the assignment of time for riding must be fair, and the division of expenses must be fair. In many partnerships, fair is fifty-fifty. Each partner does half the necessary work, gets half the riding time (whether she uses it or not), and pays half the costs. In other partnerships, fair may be something else. Partners may work out any division they choose in each of the areas where sharing is necessary. An altered percentage in one area may lead to a different alteration in another.

Sharing Work

Since work is usually the key to affordable horsekeeping, there will probably be plenty of it for the partners to divide up. Partners should write down everything that will have to be done, assess each item for the time required and the difficulty involved, then try to divide it up evenly. This will require analysis and negotiation. For example, feeding is easier and much more fun than mucking stalls and, although each has to be done one or more times a day, they can't be directly equated. Give them—and everything else—comparative values, then see if each partner is capable of doing an equal amount of work.

All aspects of a sharing arrangement have to be negotiated ahead of time, including expenses, use, and work.

If not, one partner will have to do more than the other, but that person then earns points for one or more of the other areas that sharing is necessary. For example, the person who mucks and feeds five days a week should either get more riding time or pay less than the person who only does two days a week.

Sharing Use

If you and your partner have different work or school schedules, there may be little conflict in scheduling riding time. Otherwise, you will probably have to negotiate riding time. If you both want Saturday morning, either the person who works more gets it or you may have to flip a coin for it. Remember that most horses are capable of working several hours a day, especially if they get a rest in the middle. Both partners can get a ride each Saturday, as long as the partner who goes first is reasonable and fair.

In this area, as in most others in horse sharing, it's important to know what you plan to do before the horse is in the barn. Be realistic. If riding time is likely to be a point of bitter conflict between you and your partner, each of whom is convinced she wants to ride all day Saturday and no other day, you should not enter into a partnership arrangement with each other. You should each find somebody else.

Sharing Expenses
Since you are probably sharing horse ownership primarily to cut costs, you and a partner must know before acquiring a horse exactly where each of you stands on financial matters. Find out how much money is available for horse care, even if you hope not to have to spend so much. Don't assume a best-case scenario, where you happily give up all your clothes budget, half your grocery budget, and count on telephone bills going down. Decide how much each of you will really have, month in and month out, for horsekeeping.

After you have a money figure, you have to develop a consensus with your partner about what is affordable and what isn't in the various aspects of horsekeeping. This involves searching for and pricing housing possibilities, vets, horseshoers, and equipment. Again, shop before you buy. You don't have to actually rent a stall or schedule a farrier before you have the horse, but you must know what's really available and what it's going to cost. Make sure that each of you is happy with the decisions you make and that your partner, after accepting a $100-a-month barn where both of you have to work, decides later that she wants a $300-a-month full-service barn that you can't afford.

You next have to decide what percentage each of you will pay. If it's anything other than fifty-fifty, try to assure yourself (if you are the one paying the higher percentage) that you are not going to resent it later. If your partner doesn't have as much money as you do and you agree to pay more than half the costs, you should get an additional benefit, whether it's less work or more riding time. Do the same for your partner if the situation is reversed. You may not resent paying more for the same benefits during the exciting first days of horse ownership, but you will later.

Making sure that each partner pays the agreed percentage of expenses can sometimes be difficult. Some people are more casual about bills and budgets than others, and a conscientious partner can be frustrated by a slow-paying one. If you suspect there may be a problem, you and your partner can open a joint bank account earmarked for horse expenses, with money deposited in advance according to your agreed percentage of costs. You will still have to prod a reluctant payer to come up with money, but presumably you won't have to do it so often.

INSURANCE

Do you need insurance on a co-owned horse? See Chapter 13 for thoughts on equine insurance and the low-cost horse. In general, you are probably not going to want to spend money on mortality insurance on a low-priced horse that you share with somebody else. Medical insurance makes more sense, but at the moment it's almost impossible to buy medical insurance without a mortality policy.

HORSE SHARING

Liability insurance is something else. Most homeowner's and umbrella liability policies do cover animals owned for pleasure purposes, but you must check with your insurance agent or company to make sure that your policy is not an exception. The fact of co-ownership may also affect coverage. Your agent may tell you that the horse should be formally owned by one of you to assure liability coverage.

SHOULD THE PARTNERSHIP BE IN WRITING?

According to the laws of most states, unwritten contracts are as valid as written ones for everything except real estate transactions. Still, it makes sense to put down each aspect of your partnership agreement in writing. The record may not eliminate arguments, but it should reduce their number. It will also clarify your arrangement.

You don't need a lawyer unless you are contracting to share an expensive horse. A straightforward listing of the points you've worked out should be enough. After you've written it out, make a copy for each of you.

C H A P T E R

F O U R

Horse Leasing

Strictly speaking, you don't own a horse that you lease, but leasing is an alternative worth considering if you can't find an animal you want to buy at a price you can afford to pay. You will probably find that you feel every bit as close to and proud of a leased horse as an owned one.

With horses, leasing and owning are much more alike than are renting and owning inanimate objects like houses or cars or pianos. The horse, being a living and thinking creature, responds to the person who rides and cares for him. He has no idea who actually owns him, and he will invariably accept whoever he sees most often as his person.

But while leasing can provide almost all of the benefits of ownership, it doesn't necessarily come with a lower pricetag. In some circumstances, leasing does indeed cost less than owning. In others, the cost is essentially the same. In some situations, it will cost you more to lease than to own. To determine where you fit, you have to analyze your circumstances in relation to potential leases.

WHERE TO FIND A LEASE

Look in the same places you did for giveaway or low-cost horses. The classified sections of regional horse publications often have listings devoted to leases, and cards offering leases regularly appear on the bulletin boards of feed stores and tack shops.

Boarding stables are excellent sources of leads, since an owner who is fond enough of his horse to want to keep him often prefers that he remain in his familiar barn. Call or visit every stable in your area and tell the manager what you're looking for.

THE USUAL ARRANGEMENT

Any arrangement agreeable to the owner (the lessor) and the person who wants use of the horse (the lessee) can be negotiated, but experienced horse people understand the typical lease to be this: the owner retains ownership of the horse, but he gives over his use to the lessee. The lessee may or may not have to pay a rental fee, but he will definitely have to pay normal expenses, including board, feed, shoeing, and routine veterinary care. The lease almost always has a term, whether it is a year, six months, or a show season.

Everything else in the lease depends on the expectations and the negotiating abilities of the people involved. But before you worry about getting the best deal in a particular lease, you have to decide if any kind of leasing is a good idea for you.

HORSE LEASING
WHEN TO LEASE

Leasing is rarely the only alternative for would-be owners, although it may be for people who live in the middle of huge urban areas. A shortage of nearby stabling may force a city dweller to make an arrangement with somebody who already has a stall. If so, move ahead to the section on making a good deal in your lease arrangement. Everybody else should be able to answer yes to one or more of the following questions before embarking on a lease.

Are You Unsure about Horse Ownership?
Leasing will allow you to sample the pleasures and burdens of ownership without committing too much money. But you should try to find a short-term lease if you think you might grow bored with horsekeeping. A year's lease, even at a low fee, can run up substantial maintenance bills, while a three or six months' lease will commit you to much less expense for boarding, only two or three farrier's bills and worming payments, and possibly no routine veterinary costs.

Do You Want a Better Horse than You Can Pay for?
Even well-to-do people who don't need to cut costs in other aspects of horsekeeping become involved in horse leasing, usually when they want to compete effectively in an equine sport or a particular discipline for a season or two. Someone who can't (or doesn't want to) pay $50,000 for an open amateur show jumper is willing to pay $5,000 plus expenses to show a similar horse for a season.

But even people with less lofty ambitions find themselves leasing. If you want a healthy, fully trained, ready-to-go trail horse who's healthy enough for hours of riding daily, and you want all of that on a tight budget, you might find a better deal in a leased horse. Just make sure that any monthly payments don't add up to more than the value of the horse figured over the period of time you expect to be keeping that or another similar horse.

Do You Want to Try a New Discipline?

If you think, but aren't sure, that you want to try jumping, consider a short lease on a good jumper rather than embarking on a long search for an affordable one. A leased polo pony or two will teach you more about the sport and give you more playing time than you'll get if you search the Quarter Horse tracks, then try to train the prospects you acquire. Look for prospects after you're sure the sport is for you.

WHAT LEASING COSTS

Like other kinds of horsekeeping, leasing can cost anything from a little to a lot, depending on the quality of the horse, the work you're willing to do, how good you are at negotiating, and the region of the country you live in. You will probably find that you have a little less flexibility in how and where you keep the horse, since most owners want to have a say. You may also find that the owner requires certain expenses, such as mortality insurance, that you might not opt for with your own horse.

The Free Lease

Some owners offer free leases. "Free" means only that there is no monthly or yearly fee; you will still have to pay normal maintenance costs. The quality of horses offered on free leases tends to be higher than for giveaway horses, since the owner thinks enough of the animal to retain ownership.

A free lease may or may not be a bargain, depending on the obligations that the owner imposes. A horse leased without charge that has to be kept in his own $700-a-month stall is hardly affordable, while one that can be taken to a more modest boarding stable may be.

Free leases tend to come from people or organizations that use their horses during only part of the year, usually summer. Summer camps often offer their horses on a nine months' lease from September to May, and ask only that you bring them back at the beginning of June. A camp horse should prove to be sturdy, good natured, and easy to handle. He may need a couple of weeks of vacation in September to recover from the rigors of too much affection, but he should be fully usable the rest of the nine months. Horse publications sometimes carry ads for these leases, but you may call camps directly to ask if you can lease one of their horses for the off season.

Other free leases show up in the classified ads in August and September, usually offered by people going back to school who know they won't be able to do much riding until the following summer. These leases generally come with more strings attached than do camp leases, but you can find good-quality horses among them.

The Lease for a Fee

With a lease that requires a periodic payment in addition to maintenance costs, you have another item to figure into your analysis as you determine whether the deal is really affordable. The better the horse, the more likely there is to be a fee involved. Moreover, the better the horse, the more likely the owner is to specify potentially expensive services, such as worming done by a vet rather than the lessee, a farrier visit every four weeks rather than every six or eight, and lessee-paid insurance.

A very good rider or trainer—someone who can reasonably claim to add to the value of a horse in her care—might convince an owner to lower the fee or eliminate it altogether. Even so, you must take a look at the bottom-line fee and the financial obligations that come with the particular lease to see if you can't do better for a horse of similar quality with another kind of ownership. If you decide you can do better but still like the horse offered in the lease, show your figures to the owner. He may negotiate the fee or the required expenses downward.

THE LEASE AGREEMENT

A lease for a horse is a legal contract, and you should be careful to protect yourself. It should be in writing, signed by both parties, and it should be extremely clear. If the lease involves serious money—a long-term deal for a valuable horse that has to be kept at an expensive stable—you should consider consulting a lawyer who specializes in equine subjects. You'll find ads in the horse publications.

Do-it-yourselfers should take a look at the following book for information, detailed examples, and blank forms for typical leases:

Legal Forms, Contracts and Advice for Horse Owners by Sue Ellen Marder (Breakthrough Publications, 1991)

The author is a lawyer and horsewoman, and her sample

You can use a lease form from a book, consult a lawyer, or draw up your own. Just make sure that it includes rights, obligations, and contingencies.

forms include all the common and necessary items that should appear in horse leases.

Any item in a lease can be negotiated, but most of them will include these provisions:

The Parties
The lessor and lessee should be named, as should the name of the horse involved. Most leases also include a fairly detailed description of the horse. If the horse is to be shown, the

description should include details necessary to his eligibility, such as registration, age, etc.

Length of Lease

Terms can have a specific beginning and ending date, or they can be open-ended. They should give you the means to end the agreement, and it's to the lessee's benefit to be able to end it on as short a notice as possible.

Payment

How much you will pay and when payments are due should be included. If it's to be a free lease, you may want to include that fact.

Board

This is where the owner specifies housing arrangements. He may also include feed requirements, shoeing, veterinary costs, and other aspects of care. Obviously, the less the owner specifies, the more flexibility you have in looking for low-cost alternatives. You should also make sure that the agreement is clear on who is obligated for other than routine farrier and veterinary care. A lessee might be willing to be responsible for yearly vaccinations, but few would want to take on the obligations for $2,000 worth of colic surgery.

Insurance

A valuable horse should be insured, but whether lessor or lessee pays is up for negotiation. If there is no mortality insurance, you want to make sure you are not liable for the cost of the horse if it dies (through no fault of your own or otherwise) during the term of the lease.

Use

The lease may specify how and how much the horse is to be used, whether it can be trailered to shows, whether anybody but the lessee can ride it. Although use limitations don't directly affect costs, you can sometimes agree to more limitations on use in exchange for a lower fee.

THE PARTIAL LEASE

You may find a good horse offered on a partial lease, usually half but sometimes less. In these cases, you get use of the horse for a specified percentage of the week in exchange for half (or less) of the costs of keeping the horse. As in a full lease, each item is negotiable, and a fee may or may not be charged.

You generally have less responsibility and less work in a partial lease, but you also have less to say about the care and handling of the horse and less ability to cut costs in the areas of maintenance and boarding.

A partial lease can give you lots of riding for less money than you would pay for either renting a horse or owning one. But for people who like to care for their horses as much as they like to ride them, and for people who like to visit their horses on the spur of the moment, a partial lease can be frustrating.

PART II

Keeping Your Horse

CHAPTER FIVE

The Backyard Horse

Unless you find an arrangement where you can barter your labor for board (more on that in Chapter 8), you will find that keeping your horse on your own property will be the cheapest way to house it. But it won't necessarily be the best, and it may bring more problems than you ever expected. Moreover, it may not save as much money as you think it will.

Still, you will certainly consider backyard horsekeeping if you're serious about saving money. If your backyard includes dozens of acres of farmland and a solid barn, your decision will be easy. The choice is more difficult for the rest of us.

· One thing that shouldn't figure into your decision-making process is the fact that "backyard horse" is one of the favorite epithets of snobby horse owners who board their own animals in expensive stables. Anybody who's serious about low-cost horse ownership will have to develop a thick skin for snob protection. Remember another fact before worrying too much about being looked down on for owning a "backyard horse." A horse owned by a person who uses such a term probably thinks the stall mucker is his owner, while the real owner suffers regular pangs of guilt because he sees the horse only once or twice a week.

Don't allow concerns about snobbery to affect your decision. There are plenty of other pros and cons to keep you busy.

HOW TO DECIDE WHETHER TO KEEP A HORSE AT HOME

The decision to board or to keep at home is often made for you. If your home is a city apartment, you won't be able to keep a horse in the spare bedroom. If home is a suburban subdivision, your neighbors may not be pleased by the sight of a horse grazing your lawn down to the dirt and the smell of your manure pile.

You have some serious thinking to do when there *is* room behind the house or next to the garage. To do the right thing for you and your horse, you have to make a careful and honest evaluation of your situation.

In fact, your first step in the decision-making process will be to go back and reexamine your first conclusion—that you do indeed have room to keep a horse. Adopt a skeptical frame of mind, then ask yourself these questions about your property.

Is It Legal for Horses?
Except for remote and rural areas, you are going to have to consider zoning regulations. Even if a previous resident owned horses and built elaborate stables to house them, you

cannot assume that it's automatically legal for you to do the same. The previous owner may have been violating zoning laws, or he may have been allowed to keep the horses he already owned under a "grandfather" clause that might not apply to subsequent residents. Or he may have been lucky enough that no neighbors complained.

Some communities prohibit horses altogether, but these are relatively rare. You are more likely to run into a maze of requirements that are more discouraging than prohibitive. Zoning regulations may require a specific amount of land per horse, or a specific distance between a horse pasture and neighboring houses. They may require you to obtain a special permit that spells out how you plan to handle manure disposal. They may require a particular kind of fencing.

Every community has different rules. Check with the planning office of your city or town government to find out what may affect you. You will usually find the zoning office at city or town hall, but zoning regulations may be handled by the mayor's office or town manager's office. Don't assume that because you don't find a listing for a zoning or planning office, your community has no rules. Check before you commit to horsekeeping.

If you find that you and your property don't quite qualify, you can ask for a variance from the regulations. If your property is almost suitable, you might get the variance directly from the zoning office with no further problems. But even a turndown can be taken another step—to a zoning appeals board. Most zoning appeals boards consist of ordinary people, either appointed or elected, and unless your neighbors mount a concerted campaign against you and your horse, you stand a good chance of winning a variance. You may have to ask specifically about the appeals process when you're turned down for a permit. The zoning office may not volunteer the information.

Do You Have Enough Acreage?
You may have enough property to qualify for horsekeeping according to the zoning laws while not having nearly enough to keep a horse healthy and happy. In my town, for example, you need one acre per horse. Good horsekeeping might be

Your backyard horse will graze a too-small paddock down to nothing quickly, forcing him to search for greener pastures on the other side of the fence.

managed with three acres for three horses, but one acre for one horse really isn't enough, regardless of what the zoning office says. After you allow for house, driveway, stable, and lawn, that one horse gets very little space.

While a single horse can get a reasonable amount of grazing, fresh air, and exercise on three-quarters of an acre, it can't be the same three-quarters of an acre at all times. Grass turns to mud very quickly under a horse's hooves, becoming unsightly and nearly unusable. Bacteria and parasites may develop in accumulated droppings, and pastures should be rested to stop the life cycle of these pests. Overgrazing also destroys grass, so turnout areas have to be rotated to provide forage for their residents.

A horse can certainly subsist on less than an acre, but his optimum health and happiness require more. To be fair, many boarding stables often have insufficient turnout space too. You may find that your actual grazing space compares favorably with that of the local stable. In that case, neither of you has an advantage in this category.

Can My Property Handle Horses?

You need shelter, access, and running water. In temperate climates, a run-in shed may be sufficient protection from wind and cold. See Chapter 6 for information on full-time pasture horsekeeping. If you live in a particularly cold climate, or if you want to reduce the time you have to devote to horse cleaning, you will need a barn or stable that secures the horse at night or during bad weather.

If you hope to turn a structure into a stable, or if you plan to build a brand-new one, you have to go back to the zoning office to get approval and a permit. You may also need a permit to upgrade an existing stable for modern horsekeeping.

Whichever route you go for horse housing, there are a few basic requirements. Box stalls are no longer a luxury for a favored few horses. All stabled horses deserve a chance to move around and lie down at will.

Flooring must be safe and well drained. A barn already wired for electricity must be inspected by a good electrician and repaired, if necessary, before a single horse is moved in. The building should also be accessible to large vehicles, both for horse pickup and delivery and for deliveries of feed and bedding.

Access to running water is vital. A non-polluted pond (if such a thing is possible in your area) might provide sufficient drinking water for a horse at pasture. But you'll need city or well water for inside water buckets and for other purposes— washing the stalls, equipment, barn floor, and the horse. You'll find you need an enormous amount of water for proper horsekeeping. Don't imagine you can carry enough buckets of water from the house to do these chores adequately. It will be so painful that you'll find yourself neglecting the work and neither you nor your horse will be happy.

Major renovations or construction of a new building will probably require professional design and assistance. You will find ads for contractors who specialize in livestock shelter in horse and farm publications. Your local farm bureau may also supply leads. If you're thinking about building a new barn, you will find this book valuable, both for suggested plans and construction advice:

Complete Plans for Building Horse Barns Big and Small by Nancy Ambrosiano and Mary Harcourt (Breakthrough, 1989)

Before contracting for expensive construction, consider the installation of a portable stable or barn. These modular structures aren't exactly cheap, but they do have money-saving characteristics: they require less ground preparation and foundation work and they are often taxed by your town or county at a much lower rate. Movable barns are also advertised widely in horse newspapers and magazines.

Is the Turnout Space Safe?

Some valuable horses are never turned out into pastures, but horses who spend their entire lives alternating between stall confinement and being ridden are living unnatural and possibly unhappy lives. They are also much more likely to develop vices, both in the stall and under saddle.

All horses need turnout at least some of the time, and turnout requires good fences. You may have solid existing fencing or fencing that needs only minor repair. If so, you're lucky. Horse-proof fencing is expensive, especially if you have it installed by a fencing contractor. Expect to pay between $2 and $8 a linear foot, depending on the kind of fencing you choose.

Prices for the different kinds of fencing vary widely. Your proximity to the factory that produces the fencing is a major factor in the cost, as is the cost of installation in your area. Reject barbed wire out of hand, then consider the other widely used kinds of livestock fencing. In general, fencing made of recycled tires is cheapest, as well as being safe, long lasting, and easily maintained. Unfortunately, it also looks like you have a fence made of tires. But many horse owners are willing to overlook appearance for utility.

Wire mesh fencing comes next in price, with diamond

mesh slightly more expensive than rectangular, followed by traditional board, and then PVC board. Consult with a fencing contractor about prices and suggestions for your area. Even if you feel you can do the work yourself, you'll need to find a source of materials.

Is There a Place to Use the Horse?

Property without rideable access to trails will require space for schooling or hacking. Otherwise, you're going to have to load the horse into a trailer every time you want to use him. This may not seem like a problem until you've struggled through trailering every day for three weeks. The boarding stable that stands on the edge of a trail system will begin to look very appealing.

If you've answered yes to the questions about your property, you may move on to the other aspects of backyard horsekeeping. Be prepared to deal with these additional requirements, some involving your horse and some involving you.

HORSE CARE

Depending on the circumstances, either a boarded horse or a backyard animal may get better and more attentive care. The quality of his care depends on who's able to do the caring at each place.

The backyard horse should have the best deal in terms of personalized care, since his owner is close at hand at least half of every 24-hour period. But a backyard horse owned by a person with a full-time job often gets little attention. A boarded horse may be handled more often each day simply because more people are around.

If you are deciding between a particular boarding stable and backyard care, check the stable for the number of people around during the day. Find out how much time the employees spend with each horse. Add your own time when you visit the horse to ride or groom him, and compare this to the time you could devote to your horse at home.

A backyard owner with limited time should try to enlist friends and relatives for regular visits. They won't necessarily have to do any work, but a glance into a stall or out into a paddock can help spot cast horses, colic, or opened latches before serious problems develop.

Also remember that you will have nobody to call on for opinions and advice if you're keeping your horse at home. In a boarding stable, you can ask more experienced people to take a look at bumps and bruises and runny noses to see if you really need an expensive vet call. You'll also have access to tips on training and handling.

In general, extremely inexperienced people should never attempt home horsekeeping without having spent some time around a barn. If you feel that backyard care is the only thing you can afford, consider paying for a couple of months of board first. Spend every minute you can around the barn for those months, then bring your horse home. The board money will be well spent.

SATISFYING THE HERDING INSTINCT

Given their choice, few horses would ever be alone. The strong herding instinct probably developed from the wild horse's nature as prey. As tasty herbivores, they needed company for protection, to both detect and confuse predators. The modern horse doesn't need equine protection, but he still loves and needs company.

The solitary backyard horse will be much happier with another animal around most of the time. An owner who spends a great deal of time with his horse—and this means several hours a day—might qualify, but most horses will want something with four legs. Another horse would be ideal, if there is enough space to keep him and money to feed him. A pony will do just as well, and he won't need nearly as much space and feed as a horse.

Horses can learn to enjoy the company of many other

All horses need companionship. Another horse is best, but a different animal might do.

animals, including dogs, burros, and goats—none of which require much in the way of care. Cats and horses usually get along extremely well, and a couple of barn cats will also save your grain from being nibbled by rodents.

TIME DEMANDS

The full care of even one horse requires an enormous amount of work. Every stabled horse needs hands-on care at least twice a day. Each session will include checking the horse and feeding grain or hay. A stabled horse will have his feet cleaned once a day and his stall picked out once a day. Ideally, the horse should be checked once more, and fed a third time if he's not turned out to pasture. The horse who spends most or all of his time at grass should still be handled and checked at least once a day, with supplemental feedings being given at least twice a day.

The work isn't particularly difficult, although it can be exhausting. The problem with the work involved in horse care is not so much that it's hard, but that it is relentless. It has to be done day in and day out, with no exceptions for holidays or hospitalization. If you have any doubt about your ability to live up to the time demands, you should opt for another kind of horsekeeping.

Even home horsekeepers who expect no problems finding time for the work should develop a circle of trusted friends they can ask (or pay) to take over the chores in emergencies. The best source of occasional help will be other people in similar situations—backyard horse owners who will do a favor for you in exchange for you doing one for them. Join the local horsemen's association, the state Horse Council, or any other organization that includes people who can help you. The dues are usually minimal and the people you meet may prove to be invaluable.

DEALING WITH MANURE

The average full-sized horse produces as much as fifty pounds of droppings a day. His piles will be located anywhere he travels, including the field where he grazes, the stall where he lives the rest of the time, and the pathways between the two. The pathway and stall manure should be removed every day and placed in a holding area. The field droppings can be left for a while, but eventually you will have to collect or spread them in an area where they will have a few months to lose their parasites.

You are going to have to have a manure pit, a holding structure, or a place to pile droppings and soiled bedding. It should be convenient to the barn so you don't have to travel too far with a wheelbarrow, but it should be as much out of sight and smell as possible. You will also need access for a truck if you plan to have it hauled away. Your manure pit doesn't have to be elaborate, but it should prevent the material from going where it's not wanted, and it should be located in a well-drained area.

The cheapest way to deal with manure is to find somebody who will collect it and possibly even pay you for it. Mushroom growers are particularly fond of horse manure. Next best is a grower who won't pay but will come to haul it away. Your local Cooperative Extension office may be able to give you leads to farmers who need manure. Unfortunately, many commercial users of horse manure insist that any bedding mixed in with the droppings be wheat straw or peat moss, two of the more expensive kinds of bedding.

You must plan for manure storage and disposal before you move a horse onto your property. If you don't have the space for manure, you don't have the space for a horse.

You may also compost your own manure, both to improve your own soil and to sell or give to other people. Again, Cooperative Extension or a Soil Conservation office should be able to offer information on composting. Once the manure is composted—which can happen in a few months—the material will fill up only about one-third the space it did previously, and it can be spread easily and attractively anywhere. Even pine shavings and low-priced forms of straw bedding will compost sufficiently for home use, although they will take a little longer than peat moss or wheat straw to break down into a soil-like material.

To compost, you're going to need enough space for long, low rows of manure in which you will make depressions to catch rain. How long it will take to decompose depends on the percentage of droppings and bedding. The less bedding, the quicker the composting. Decomposition can be hurried along by adding nitrogen sources such as urea or cottonseed meal and by soaking the pile regularly to moisten it all the way to the bottom.

The determined affordable horsekeeper can even make money from manure. A man in my area fills empty feed sacks with finished horse manure compost and sells it for $3 a bag to home gardeners. That's certainly better than paying somebody to haul the unfinished stuff away.

C H A P T E R

S I X

Pasture Keeping

![divider]

Call it full-time turnout, pasture board, grass keeping, or field keeping. Whichever name you choose, it means one thing: a horse who lives outdoors all the time. You can provide pasture living on your own property or you can pay for it, but in either case, it's likely to be the cheapest and often the healthiest way you can keep your horse.

Pasture board on someone else's property should cost you between $50 and $80 a month when no supplemental feeding is necessary. Add $25 or so monthly for the addition of hay, and a little more than that if grain is also fed. On your own property, you obviously pay no monthly charge for the use of the pasture, but you are going to have to borrow or rent a tractor for the occasional removal or spreading of manure. You will probably have to supply a certain amount of feed (more on that later), but during much of the year you will be paying a smaller feed bill for the pastured horse.

THE AFFORDABLE HORSE

Keeping a horse at pasture is certainly cheapest, but does it meet the needs of you and your horse?

Most horses, given a choice between the most luxurious stall and the barest pasture, would choose the pasture. They wouldn't even stop to think about it. Owners do have to think about it, since pasture keeping isn't suitable for every horse. You or the person you pay to keep your horse has to provide more than a fenced pasture.

REQUIREMENTS OF PASTURE KEEPING

The needs of the pastured horse are similar to those of the stabled horse, although these needs are met in different ways. Both horses need shelter, feed, water, and company.

Shelter

Wild horses make do with a stand of trees or brush for protection from cold winds and rain. We like to do a little better by our horses, but even so, the full-time pasture resident doesn't need much in the way of shelter.

A simple three-sided shed is sufficient, provided it has space for every horse in the field. Each horse should have enough room to turn around and to lie down, roughly 100 square feet per animal. You will need additional room if you plan to put the feed and water buckets inside the shed and even more space if you intend to store hay in the structure.

The shed should be located on a well-drained area of the pasture, and its opening usually faces south for greatest warmth. Some horsekeepers will provide bedding in the shed so the horses can rest comfortably. The bedding won't have to be changed nearly as often as stall bedding, since the horses will spend very little time inside the shelter. Many

Full-time pasture residents need only a simple shelter, but it must be large enough to handle all the horses at the same time.

horses prefer to lie down outside, so you don't have to worry about bedding for them once you identify their preferences.

Feed
In the wild, horses live on the grasses they forage. In theory, pastured domestic horses can do the same. In reality, however, domestic horses are usually confined to a relatively limited area. When grass supplies are poor, they don't have the option of setting off on a five-mile trek to a better source of supply.

How much supplemental feed a horse needs depends on the season, the size of his pasture, the quality of the grass, the amount of work the horse does, and his own physical characteristics. Working out a supplemental feeding program requires a certain amount of experimentation, but there are general guidelines you can follow.

In regions where freezing temperatures are common in winter, you can be assured that you are going to have to supply additional feed during the winter months. In climates where the thermometer rarely drops below freezing, your horse may manage on pasture grass in winter, but you may also find out that your pastures burn out badly in summer and the horse needs additional feed then.

Whenever grass is growing well, a turned-out horse can obtain all or a good part of his nutrients from his pasture, as long he has enough grass for his exclusive use. Experts have different opinions on this, but you can figure you need at least two acres per horse of good, growing pasture to provide all or most of what he needs. You may get by with less if your grass is particularly rich in nutrients, but you will need more in poor-quality pasture. Your local Cooperative Extension office can help you identify and analyze the grasses in your pasture.

If you expect your horse to do more than limited work, he may need more calories than he can get from grass, even with all-day grazing. Having to tighten the girth one notch more or seeing the outline of his ribs will signal you to supplement the horse's grazing with small meals of grain two or three times a day. If the horse is boarded in someone else's pasture and you are unable to supplement his feed, you should look for another kind of housing arrangement for your horse.

Some healthy unworked horses or very lightly worked horses are also unable to keep on enough weight in spite of good pasture. Check and float teeth first, since they may not be grazing efficiently. If there is no dental problem, observe the horse in the field. Because of his personality, he may be working himself a little too hard in the field and burning off more calories than he can take in from grazing. He may require supplemental feeding year round, or you may decide that he is unsuited to pasture keeping.

A horse who has been stabled and fed prepared grain and hay should not be suddenly turned out to feed himself. Some will manage just fine, but others may suffer digestive upset from the change. Get the horse gradually used to an all or mostly grass diet by continuing to feed, in smaller amounts, the same food he is accustomed to. Over the course of a few days, you can cut him down to whatever level of additional feed you've decided upon.

Water
Pastured horses need a constant supply of free-choice water. A clean stream or a spring-fed pond is ideal, but water can be brought by pipe or hose to a trough. Carrying enough bucketed water for more than a couple of horses will be backbreaking work. During freezing weather, you have to make sure that water remains accessible, whether by breaking ice, providing an electric heater, or carrying water from the barn or house.

Company
Horses like the company of other horses, and they like it most of all when they live outdoors. A stabled horse sees enough other animals, whether cats, dogs, people, or other horses, to have his herding instinct satisfied. A pasture-kept horse has far less human and pet companionship and will be a very lonely creature without another animal sharing his pasture. The herding instinct is so strong that many people

Pasture-boarded horses need a regular supply of water.

are convinced that it is cruel to keep a single horse outdoors without regular company.

The occasional unsociable animal seems to adjust well to solitary living, but most horses are highly social and need to see and smell pasture mates. Sometimes, a horse is satisfied with the regular sight of a horse in another paddock if that is all you can offer him.

WHICH HORSES DO WELL AT PASTURE?

Not every horse is suited to full-time pasture life. Certain psychological and physical characteristics can make a horse thrive on pasture living or turn him into an unhappy, uncomfortable animal. How you plan to use the horse also plays a role in his success in the pasture.

Personality

The extremely bold and the extremely timid horse often do poorly when kept full-time outdoors in the company of other horses. The bold horse feels he must be boss of the pasture and sometimes loses condition by concentrating too hard on maintaining his position. The timid horse is sometimes bossed so aggressively by every other horse that he fails to defend himself, suffering regular bites and kicks. He also loses out on supplemental feeding unless an effort is made to feed the herd out of separate buckets.

Every group of horses will have a top boss and a lowest-level follower, but these two will do well if their tendencies are not too extreme. Only when their personalities harm their health and condition should they be considered poor candidates for pasture keeping.

Age

Old horses are probably most likely to be turned out full time, since many owners use pasture board as an inexpensive way to maintain a retired animal. Outdoor living is sometimes harder on older horses than on young ones, since many aging horses need extra calories to maintain weight, suffer more than younger horses from cold weather, and are sometimes bullied by more active animals.

Whether pasture keeping is unsuited to a particular horse depends on the nature of the individual, the climate, and the personalities of his herd mates. Any horse has to be watched closely for the first few days and weeks of a turnout situation, but the older horse should be watched even more closely and checked more often.

Coat

Every candidate for pasture keeping should be able to grow a good, healthy coat. The need is most obvious for the horse who lives in an area with cold winters, but it's also important that a horse have an adequate coat even in summer.

A reasonable summertime hair covering will help protect the pasture-kept horse from both sunburn and flies, either of which can cause great pain and annoyance. Most outdoor horses will use their shelters during the worst part of the day for fly and sun protection, but some neglect to get themselves under cover.

Hair coat is even more important in the winter, of course, and a horse who doesn't grow a thick one is simply unsuited to pasture keeping in cold climates. Unfortunately, you can't always tell what kind of coat a horse is going to grow until you can observe him through a winter.

As you look for an affordable horse that you intend to keep outdoors, you can take some steps to predict the kind of coat he grows. You can ask a previous owner, certainly, but the owner may tell you he doesn't know. He may have clipped the horse every October, reclipped in January, and never saw the real coat. The horse may have been kept stabled all day long and grew only half the coat he would have outdoors. Or the horse may have been blanketed day and night and never grew a winter coat at all.

You can predict with occasional accuracy by breed. Most pony breeds grow luxuriant winter coats, as do Morgans and most breeds that have draft blood in their ancestries. This includes the warmbloods. But Thoroughbreds often grow scanty coats, and warmbloods that look like Thoroughbreds may not grow much in the way of a winter covering. The same is often true of Standardbreds. If they look like their Thoroughbred ancestors, they may not get a good coat. If they take after their Morgan and other harness-bred ancestors, they may grow plenty.

Many Arabians grow very little coat, although there are plenty of exceptions. Quarter Horses and Appaloosas vary, but most do well outdoors regardless of the coat lengths. A horse who doesn't grow enough coat can stay outside in moderate climates, but he should be stabled during especially cold periods.

USING THE PASTURE-KEPT HORSE

Many owners utilize pasture keeping for horses they don't use. Retired horses are kept outdoors, as are sporting horses during their off season. Hunters are often turned out during spring and summer; polo ponies are turned out during the winter. But you can pasture-board a horse that you use regularly, although you will have to do a little more work than you would with a stabled animal.

Catching
Horses vary in their willingness to be caught and brought in from their pasture, regardless of the percentage of their days they spend outdoors. But you will likely find that a horse who is already difficult to catch will become even more so if he lives outdoors full time. One who is easy to bring into his stable after an allotted two hours of turnout becomes an evasive imp when he is brought in just to work.

The more horses live according to their natural instincts,

Pasture dwellers can become more difficult to catch than other horses, but most can be taught to tolerate being haltered if you bring a little grain to them. Photo: Timothy Chaucer

the less willing they often are to adjust their instincts to accept human handling. They don't exactly forget how to behave, but they sometimes pretend that they don't have to do what they are told. Most will behave perfectly well once they're caught and saddled. It's the catching that is the challenge.

A little grain works wonders for the horse who lives mostly on pasture grass. Bring it in a bucket, and eventually you will be able to bring an empty bucket to lure the horse. With any luck, someday you'll be able to catch him without the bucket.

A haltered horse is easier to catch, but a halter does present a danger to an unsupervised horse. The halter can catch on a branch, a nail in a fence, or a hoof being used to scratch a face. If you feel you must leave a halter on the horse to control him when you want to use him, make sure it's a halter that will break away if the horse catches it on something in the pasture.

Cleaning

A horse who lives outdoors becomes remarkably dirty, since he lies down to roll and sleep as often as a stabled horse does. Many horses are especially fond of mud for rolling. The grooming that has to be done is mostly for you, rather than him. His health doesn't require more than a removal of heavily caked mud so that skin problems don't develop. He will also need a hoof cleanout every couple of days. If he's unshod, the hooves rarely retain mud and manure anyway.

But your comfort in riding requires more grooming than that. You are going to want to remove all dirt from the areas where the equipment touches the horse's body as well as from the areas you are likely to touch while riding or petting him. You must be careful not to groom too thoroughly, though. In summer, dust and mud help protect a horse from biting flies. In winter, dirt and grease in the coat help protect against cold winds.

You are going to have to compromise on cleanliness, removing enough dirt to ensure skin health and protect your equipment but not so much that you compromise his natural insulation. You must also accept the fact that the horse will not look as slick as stabled and blanketed horses, particularly during the winter.

Cooling Out

A horse with a long natural coat gets wet easily when he exerts himself. After a strenuous ride, you must be sure to cool him by walking him under a blanket or cooler until he's dry before turning him back outside. This can take a long time, perhaps as long as the ride itself. Owners of stabled horses solve the wet winter coat problem by clipping. A stabled and blanketed hunter may get a full body clip, leaving only a saddle patch and leg hair long for protection. Other riding horses may get a trace clip along the belly, the girth area, and the chest.

A heavy-coated pasture dweller may perspire during winter work and requires blanketed cooling after being untacked.

PASTURE KEEPING

A full-time pasture dweller should not be clipped at all in extremely cold areas, but he can get a minimal trace clip in milder climates. Minimal means a patch of perhaps a couple of inches behind the forelegs where the girth goes around the belly. This small amount can save you cooling time without interfering with the horse's ability to resist cold.

Pasture keeping is more common in the British Isles than in North America, possibly because British winters tend to be warmer and summers cooler and less buggy than here. The two most helpful books that concentrate on pasture keeping are British, but each offers plenty of detailed advice that applies to horse owners on both sides of the Atlantic. You may not find them in your local bookstore, but most stores should be able to order them for you as long as they remain in print.

The Horse at Grass, prepared by the British Horse Society (Half Halt Press, 1984)

Keeping a Horse Outdoors by Susan McBane (Trafalgar Square, 1984)

C H A P T E R

S E V E N

The Boarded Horse

You will find that boarding your horse in somebody else's stable is the most expensive way to keep him. But there is so much variation in the cost of boarding between regions and between stables in the same region that you can always find bargains in boarding. Even high-priced stables in expensive regions can be affordable to a horse owner willing to negotiate and compromise.

To find the best boarding deal, you must examine the circumstances and services that make boarding expensive, then determine what you and your horse can comfortably give up. After you decide what you must have from a boarding stable, you begin your search for one that offers—and charges—for only the facilities and services that you want. Or you can negotiate with one that usually offers and charges more.

Your first step is to make a list of every boarding possibility you can find within what you feel is a reasonable driving distance, whether it's fifteen minutes, half an hour, or more. You'll find large stables advertised in the Yellow Pages, display ads of horse publications, and sometimes in newspaper classifieds. Smaller operations place their ads in local horse publications, often offering single stalls at a time. When you have a list, begin your analysis.

LOCATION

The location of a stable plays a major role in the price the owner charges for boarding. Two aspects of location will be important to you. You want your horse as close to your home as possible, and you want your horse close to a place to use him.

Proximity to Home

The closer a stable is to a population center, the higher the boarding fee is likely to be. There are two reasons for this. The expenses of operation are highest in a city or close suburb, what with the price of sufficient land, business and property taxes, licenses, manure hauling, etc. In addition, the fact that so many people live nearby increases the demand for stall space, allowing the stable operator to charge more.

The horse owner who lives in a small town or rural area has an immediate advantage in the search for an affordable stable. Other owners face a greater challenge. To expand the list of possible choices, suburban residents should broaden their ideas of what proximity really is. If you live in a suburb of a city, you tend to think of other suburbs of the same city as being near you, since you regularly hear news about them and advertising leads you to shop at their stores. You may find a stable located in a town not part of what you think of as your metropolitan area that's actually closer than one that is. You need a detailed map as you weigh the pros and cons of each stable's location.

After compiling a list of prospects, you must make an honest assessment of driving time to each and decide what it means in terms of your work or school schedule. Will you have time to see the horse after work, or will the length of the drive mean you see him only on weekends? Also think about what the time commitment will mean to your enjoyment of the horse and any work you plan to do to keep costs down. An hour's drive may not seem like much for the first few weeks, but you may begin to look on it as an endless journey once the initial thrill of ownership wears off.

Proximity to Riding

It doesn't matter how close the stable is to your home if there's no place near the stable where you can safely ride in the manner you wish. A stable that can offer access to a variety of riding possibilities will probably cost more than one with more limited facilities.

You may come across stables that offer no access to riding of any kind. These will probably be advertised as for "retirees, lay-ups, or broodmare care." This means they are unsuitable for anyone who plans active use of their horse, either because of a lack of access to trails and rings or because the owner doesn't want the work and liability of maintaining riding areas. A farm that doesn't permit riding may be suitable as a low-cost temporary home for a horse who needs several months of rest and recovery before you can begin to ride him.

More likely, you are going to want a stable with riding access immediately. The most expensive will offer everything: extensive trails, a large, lighted outdoor ring, and an indoor arena. What you really need depends on the kind of riding you intend to do. For recreational riding, access to trails is most important, and you will enjoy your riding more if you can reach those trails with little or no travel along busy roads. A stable that offers nothing but proximity to a trail system is likely to be reasonably priced, but it will provide all the riding access that most casual riders need.

For a rider who intends to take lessons and practice equitation, an outdoor ring becomes a necessity. Access to trails is not necessary if ring work is all you intend to do, but consider trail access a bonus worth a couple of points in your decision-making process. Even the most avid user of rings feels the urge to hit the trails in spring and fall.

A rider who intends to train himself or a horse for showing also needs a ring, and it should be a well-maintained one with jumps, barrels, dressage markers, or whatever you need for your discipline. Whether ring users also need an indoor arena depends on the climate and the hardiness of the rider. The horse is less fussy. He will actually prefer working in winter to summer. Only ice or deep snow prevents a horse from working outdoors, provided he's warmed up before strenuous work and cooled out properly afterwards. The rider may be less comfortable outdoors, and a training program that requires regular work may prove too difficult outdoors in a very cold climate.

Be prepared to pay plenty for boarding in a stable with a large indoor arena on the premises. If you feel that you must have indoor riding, you are going to have to be even more zealous in your efforts to save money elsewhere in the boarding process.

Nobody wants to compromise on the quality of the facilities used by his horse, but some give and take may prove necessary for affordable boarding. What you must do is compromise on items that don't matter while holding out for the best on those items that really are important.

Stalls

Standing or straight stalls, while not exactly cruel, do have an aura of Victorian austerity about them. Their inmates are tied and have neither the freedom nor the space to lie down. Most modern horse people consider a box stall nearly as important as food and water for their animals and would never accept a straight stall just to make boarding affordable. But you can compromise on the size of the stall.

The most luxurious of box stalls measure 16 by 16 feet, but a measurement of 12 by 12 is perfectly adequate for even large horses. A small horse—one of 15 hands or less—can be comfortable in a 10 by 10 stall, provided he is agile enough to get himself down and up without becoming cast against a wall.

A window turns even a small stall into luxury accommodations, at least from the horse's point of view. But a horse actually needs a window only if he gets little turnout time or suffers from allergic respiratory disease. One who spends most of his days outdoors does well in a windowless stall at night.

The walls of a stall don't need to be painted, stained, or otherwise finished. In fact, be suspicious of any that are, no matter how neat they look. Many horses like to lick and

A boarding stable doesn't need to provide fancy stalls. Clean bedding and dry, secure surroundings are plenty for a healthy and happy horse.

nibble stall boards, and there is no point in paying extra for a cosmetic enhancement that may actually endanger your horse.

Barn Condition
In assessing the condition of the barn, be careful to differentiate between superficial and structural soundness. Barns are difficult and expensive to paint, and many safe, secure ones are in desperate need of a paint job. Don't assume that a magnificent new barn is automatically safer than the one with the peeling paint.

Dampness is dangerous to horses, and any signs of leaks or poor drainage or any smell of mustiness should be investigated. Remember that even an immaculate, well-painted, and beautifully appointed barn can be damp if it was built in a low-lying spot or uses an overburdened septic system.

Faults in electrical systems can be deadly, and even a new barn is not exempt. Look for well-insulated wires and the lack of extension cords running here and there in the tack room and grooming stall. The more electrical equipment used in a barn, the greater the chance of something being left on, or shorting out, or doing something else to cause a fire.

Look for a barn with a no-smoking policy that is strictly enforced. It's best if nobody smokes anywhere in the barn or in any attached building, but if exceptions are made, they should be limited to tack rooms, offices, or somewhere else where neither horses nor feed are kept. Never put a horse you love in a barn where anybody is allowed to smoke near a stall. No matter how good the facilities and how little you pay, it won't be worth it.

Feed and Bedding

If feed and bedding are supplied as part of the boarding arrangement, their quality matters. Generally, any brand-name feed will be adequate for the horse of average health in ordinary use. As you will see in Chapter 11, the feed doesn't have to be the most expensive or the highest-protein mix available as long as it comes from a recognized feed company. In fact, a stable that charges higher board rates because it claims to feed the label with the most nutrients and protein is providing something that most horses don't need. But an operator who feeds a brand you've never heard of, or one who mixes and matches straight grains, should be questioned to make sure he has the best interests of the horses and not just economy in mind. Quality of hay also matters. Try to get a look at the hay storage in the barn you are considering. The bales should consist of leafy, reasonably fine hay with no smell or feel of moisture.

The easiest way to see if the horses at a particular stable are well fed is to take close look at several of the current residents. They should be in good flesh, neither too fat nor too thin. You should be able to feel their ribs, not see them, and their coats should be shiny in summer and thick (if not clipped) in winter. One thin horse doesn't mean a poor feeding program, two may not, but three or more almost certainly do.

Cleanliness

A clean barn is important to a horse's health and safety, but you may see cleanliness carried so far that you begin to suspect that too much time and money are going into something that doesn't affect your horse's comfort. Droppings should certainly be removed regularly from stalls, center aisles, walkways, and everywhere else the horses go. You don't want to step in manure when you go to visit your horse, and you don't want your horse packing manure into his hooves. Urine-soaked bedding has to be removed daily, and urine pools in areas outside the stalls should be hosed down.

Other kinds of dirt don't need the same kind of attention. Mud and bedding should be swept from aisles and walkways at least once a day, but a stable operator who doesn't allow a stray wisp of straw to spend more than a minute on the floor will probably charge you more than you really need to pay for adequate care for your horse. Unless you plan to visit wearing a white linen suit and matching suede shoes on a regular basis, don't spend limited boarding funds on a stable that vacuums the aisles.

SERVICES

While facilities affect the board fee, the services offered by the stable play an even greater role in the variation you'll find as you price boarding options. What the stable does for your horse determines what you pay, and owners who board horses at neighboring stables of similar size and appearance may pay dramatically different fees. Moreover, owners of horses in the same stable may pay different amounts. It all depends on what the owner wants the stable to do, and what she can do for herself.

The most basic (and cheapest) kind of board offers no services whatsoever. This may be called "stall rental" or "rough board." In some areas, rough board might include a few basic services, so you have to be sure you know what you're talking about as you study your options. Stall rental usually means that you get a stall for your horse. Sometimes you have access to a small pasture for turnout. You do all the feeding, grooming, and stall cleanup, you supply all the feed and bedding, and you may even have to store the supplies at your home. Stall rental works only if you live very close to the stable. Otherwise, you will probably find horse care too burdensome to continue for very long. For an owner who lives close to the stable, stall rental can be a tremendous bargain. You will pay only a little more than you would for pasture board in your area. Even though stabling requires a better barn, it requires less land. Figure on $75 to $125 a month, depending on your region.

The other end of the boarding spectrum is "full board," the most expensive way to go. The definition of full board can vary too, but at its most elaborate it means that everything your horse needs is supplied. Stable employees feed, groom, and turn him out. They clean his stall, give him medications, and exercise him. Some stables will tack him up when you plan to ride, then untack him and cool him out afterwards. You don't even have to visit him if you don't want to. Figure on paying $400 to $1,000 a month for all this service, more if training is added.

Other board arrangements offer any combination of these services, and you pay accordingly. Some boarding stable managers offer only one combination of services and charge one board rate. Most are willing to negotiate, however. In either case, you must assess what services you can give up and what you want the stable to provide.

Feeding

Most boarders expect the stable to both buy and distribute the feed to their horses. The owners have neither the time to feed at least twice a day nor the inclination to buy and haul hundred pound sacks of grain. But a rough-board stable might agree to have you do your own feeding with supplies you store in their feed room. Figure that an average-sized horse with minimal grazing will need at least $2 a day's worth of grain and hay. Remember that a stable that buys in bulk can usually get better deals than the person who buys for one horse, and might be able to go lower than that figure. If the stable figure is lower, or if it's even close, pay the stable to supply the feed. Each feeding is neither difficult nor time-consuming, but it has to be done so often that it can become a burden.

Stall Cleaning

Stall mucking is the worst job in the barn, and boarding stables often have trouble finding employees to do the work. Many stables are willing to have boarders clean their own stalls in exchange for a reduction in the monthly fee. Figure this way to see if a proposed reduction is reasonable. The stable will expect an employee to spend an average of fifteen minutes a day on each stall. On days when only droppings need to be removed, the time will be shorter. On days when wet bedding has to be replaced, it may take a little longer. On total bedding replacement day, it will take longer still. If the employee receives $5 an hour, that is $1.25 per stall per day. Your stall cleaning labor alone should be worth $37.50 off your board bill each month.

Do you need to clean the stall each day? You probably should, and a meticulous stable manager may insist you do. But you can probably get by with every-other-day mucking, especially if your horse spends a good part of his day outside. Let your horse be the guide, though. A manure-stained body

Most boarders can save on bills by mucking their own stalls.

and damp feet in a stabled horse are signs that his stall needs cleaning more often.

Grooming

Unless you plan to be a stranger to your horse, you don't need to pay somebody to groom him. In most climates during most of the year, a horse doesn't need daily grooming. During muddy seasons, whether winter or spring, a horse who spends time outdoors will have to have his feet cleaned out no less than every other day. Even that work can be reduced if you let him go unshod during the worst muddy seasons. His feet will thrive and you won't have to do so much work.

Nor is daily coat care an absolute necessity during much of the year. An every-other-day going over to remove caked mud, burrs, and other unpleasantries is enough for most horses. What regular grooming does do is provide a checkup of the horse's condition, an early warning of illnesses and injuries, and a socialization experience for the horse. Rather than paying a stable to groom for you, try to arrange with another boarder to trade grooming days during periods when you can't see your horse every day. Do your horse and your friend's one day, and she will do hers and yours the next. You will add only ten or fifteen minutes to your stable time on your visit, and you'll save money.

Exercise

Horses can't be expected to stay healthy and well conditioned while standing in their stalls all day long. Avoid paying for somebody to exercise your horse by using him yourself each day, by finding a stable that provides several hours of turn-out, or by making an arrangement with someone who loves to ride but can't afford a horse. Only if your horse is so difficult, so talented, or so fragile that you trust only a professional should you pay someone to ride him.

If you find yourself considering paying someone to exercise your horse, go back to Chapter 3 and think again about horse sharing. It may be more suited to your schedule than single ownership.

Other Services

Stables may offer everything from worming, to teeth floating, to vaccination clinics as part of their fees. Find out what you would be paying the stable for the services and compare what it would cost you to provide the same services to your own horse.

A stable that adds $10 a month for worming is making a 100 percent profit, since your horse needs a $10 tube of worm paste only every other month. The stable does provide the labor involved and does take over the scheduling worries, but affordable horsekeeping always means more labor and more worries.

LESSON USE

In most stables, you can negotiate fees down only so far. When you have done all you can to reduce costs and still can't manage the monthly boarding charge, you have another option. Stables that offer lessons will usually give a reduced board rate to a horse they can use for lessons.

The horse must be suitable, of course. For your own protection, don't even suggest your horse for lessons if you have any idea he might be bad tempered, nervous, or clumsy. He must be well enough trained that he responds to riders' cues in the traditional way, but horses of all levels of training beyond the basic can be useful in lessons.

Few owners want their horses used during an endless round of lessons. A conscientious instructor won't allow a horse to be abused, but enough poor riding can damage both his mouth and his mind. Don't agree to lesson use at the stable's discretion. You should negotiate for a reduced boarding fee based on how much use the horse gets. One full-hour lesson or two half-hour lessons a day five or six days a week shouldn't be harmful to a mature horse.

Find out how much the stable charges per hour lesson, then figure your horse to be worth perhaps one-third of that figure. For a $20 lesson, your horse earns about $7. If he is used in twenty-four lessons a month, you should expect $168 off your board bill. Ask for more if they plan to teach jumping or anything else that might lead to injury to the horse.

The instructors may be tempted to use him more often if he proves to be a particularly good lesson horse, but be clear and insistent that he do no more work than you want him to. However, you may find that the extra attention is good for him. If so, negotiate the board charge downward still more.

You must make sure that the stable takes care of liability insurance for your horse if he's used in lessons. See that their policy covers horses used as well as owned by them, and if you can have yourself actually named on the policy, so much the better.

Working for Board

Have you reduced the board bill as much as you can by taking over grooming, stall mucking, and other individual services your horse needs? Is the monthly charge still too high? Many stables will allow you to exchange your labor for part or even all of what you owe to keep your horse there.

Some stables won't volunteer the fact that they will barter board for labor, while others are so desperate for barn workers that they will include the possibility in classified ads. Look for phrases like "co-op board" or "working it off." Or just come right out and ask about it when you find a stable you like but can't afford.

There is no one policy followed by all or even most stables. Nor is there much consistency in what co-op labor is considered to be worth. It's up to you to work out the best deal for yourself. Most stables that do allow boarders to work off fees

Working off board bills requires negotiation of both duties and board reduction.

will negotiate with you, although some have a set policy. One large boarding and lesson stable in my area will give boarders $5 off for every hour of barn labor on horses other than their own that they complete. Boarders can do an hour a week, two hours a day, or whatever they can manage to make up for whatever they can't afford to pay for board.

WHAT KIND OF WORK IS INVOLVED?

In most cases, you will be asked to do the most unpleasant work in the barn, the kind the stable has trouble finding permanent employees to do. This includes stall mucking, raking manure piles, and hauling feed. But boarders in long-term co-op arrangements often progress to better jobs, once they have learned enough to do them. I've known people who get free board for their horse in exchange for exercising top-quality horses for richer owners. For the horse lover, that's the best of all possible worlds.

IS IT LEGAL?

Most work-for-board arrangements are "off the books," which means that no money changes hands, no income taxes are withheld or paid, and no benefits are included. It's a gray area of tax and labor law as to whether participants in such an arrangement are working for someone for pay and are therefore subject to income taxes and labor regulations.

Farming has a long history of nontraditional labor use and compensation, and there has been no appreciable effort on the part of government officials to clarify the status of arrangements like co-op board. You can ask a lawyer about the legality of the arrangement in your state.

MAKING THE DEAL

For those who decide on a direct work-for-board arrangement with no employee status, working out a fair deal is paramount. Let's automatically assume that *you* will be fair to the stable by working the hours or doing the jobs you agree to in a thorough and conscientious manner. Your concentration during the deal-making process should be on making sure the stable is fair to you. You must work out an arrangement that gives you a level of credit for your work that equals what a regular employee would cost the stable. In most cases, that means your work is worth more per hour than the stable pays its entry-level employees, usually minimum wage. Here's why your work is worth more.

Minimum Wage vs. Real Cost

In addition to rising regularly, the minimum wage varies from state to state. For the sake of illustration, say that your stable, which pays minimum wage, gives its payroll workers $4 per hour. But each employee costs his employer considerably more than $4 per hour, since the stable has to pay half his required social security contribution, a fee for worker's compensation insurance, and a tax that goes to the state's unemployment compensation fund. Medical or pension benefits, if they're provided, would add to the outlay. The stable probably spends at least $5 per hour on that $4-per-hour worker. A boarder who performs the work of that employee should expect a minimum of $5 off the board bill for each hour of work. Adjust the figure up or down, depending on what employed stable help costs at your barn or in your area.

Per Job or Per Hour?

It may be more convenient for you or the stable to base your work and your board reduction on the completion of a particular job rather than a specific number of hours. You should still figure a fair per-hour rate for the work by estimating, and averaging if necessary, how long it takes to complete.

For example, if your job is to be to maintain the bedding in half a dozen stalls, find out first what the stable believes is the standard for stall maintenance. Obviously, if bedding has to be completely changed every day, that job will take much longer than if just the soiled spots are picked every day and bedding changed only once a week. Figure the total work time for the week for all the stalls, multiply that figure by 4 1/3 for a monthly time total, then multiply the hours by $5 (or whatever hourly figure you've decided is fair). The total should be your monthly board reduction.

You are probably not going to want to muck stalls—or groom, or tack up lesson horses, or whatever job you agree to—seven days a week. You and another working boarder can do both your job and the other person's once or twice a week so you each can have a day or two off. Otherwise, you should try to negotiate a day off from the job, even if you have to pay a little extra board money.

Quality of Help
Farm owners and stable operators in all branches of the equine industry bemoan the quality of help available for

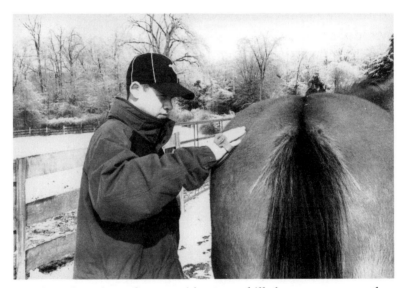

Working boarders often provide more skilled, more trustworthy, and more loving horse care than employed stable workers.

minimum wage. Understandably, many workers are reluctant to do hard, dirty, sometimes smelly work for a low salary. A horse owner who barters labor for board reduction is likely to be more qualified, more motivated, and nicer to the horses than many of the employed stable hands available in the area. Use that argument as you negotiate for your board reduction.

WHAT'S IN IT FOR YOU

At first glance, doing an hour's difficult labor for $5 off your board bill may seem like a pretty poor deal, particularly if you can find an easier part-time job elsewhere that pays you more. But it offers you benefits that even a better-paying job doesn't.

More Time with Your Horse
While most stable managers discourage co-op boarders from devoting their working time to their own horses, you do get a chance to see your horse and check up on his condition while you work. You can also do your barn work, then have your ride or do your personal horse care immediately after. With a part-time job somewhere else, you would have much more total travel time.

Learning Experiences
Every hour you spend around a barn, you learn something about horses. You can't do that at McDonald's or Macy's or at the reception desk of the dentist's office. The more a horse owner knows, the better his horse performs and the happier both horse and owner are.

A horse owner who has to watch his checkbook gets more

than a happier horse from learning. He gets the skills and knowledge to make horse ownership affordable. Take advantage of every opportunity to observe and learn. You'll have plenty of them, even if your assignment is stall mucking. Listen in when the vet pays a barn call on somebody else's horse. You'll see what ringworm looks like, or how a horse drags his front hooves when he has navicular disease, and what kind of a runny nose is serious enough for antibiotics.

Watch more experienced horse handlers to see what devices stop cribbing, what you can use to prevent stall walking, and how to pick up the feet of a tough horse without resorting to a twitch.

Working boarders should take advantage of every opportunity to learn about horse care and health from skilled horsemen and visiting professionals.

THE AFFORDABLE HORSE

The more you know, the less you have to pay somebody else to do. You will eventually save a lot more than the $5 or so off your board bill for every hour you spend around horses.

THE WORKING STUDENT

There's still another way to save on board bills, and with this method you often don't pay anything at all. Large lesson and show barns sometimes provide places for working students. The system is controversial, subject to abuse, and not suitable for everyone, but it's well established in the equine industry. Arrangements vary among barns, but a working student position often includes free board for a horse. But you will need plenty of time to spare to take advantage of this system.

At its most elaborate, a working student program may provide housing for the student, board for a horse, a small salary and benefits, plus instruction for horse and/or student. In exchange, the student works, essentially full-time, in the barn of the trainer operating the program. The work can range from entry-level barn work, to instructing beginners, to exercising show horses. It often involves traveling to shows. Individual agreements may include any or all of these benefits and duties.

Some working student relationships offer tremendous advantages to both parties. In others, the students are worked too hard, treated poorly, and receive little training. It's up to the potential student to investigate the facilities, to talk to other students, and to work out a clear understanding of the obligations of both sides, in writing if possible.

While the traditional working student arrangement involves a full-time commitment, some stables may agree to a part-time plan. One that includes board for the horse may work well for you, giving you all the benefits of co-op board in a more professional format.

Most trainers who use working students prefer people who intend to pursue careers with horses and have no other major responsibilities. This attitude tends to make the system more suitable for young people. But some trainers may consider an older adult as a suitable candidate. Working student jobs appear in horse publication classified ads, but you can often locate them by calling show barns and asking if they use working students. A few additional questions will tell you if the job will offer you what you need to keep your horse affordably in exchange for a commitment of time you can manage.

PART III

Maintaining Your Horse

Health Care

Every horse must have regular attention paid to his health. He needs preventive care and he will need treatment if he's injured or ill. There is no way to take decent care of a horse and avoid medical expenses altogether, but you can reduce them to a manageable level. You are going to have to educate yourself, shop carefully for supplies, and shop even more carefully for a veterinarian to handle situations that you can't manage yourself.

As you plan for affordable health care for your horse, remember two rules. First, never sacrifice necessary care just to save money. Second, when in doubt, call the vet. But even if you follow these rules to the letter, you can still spend far less than the average owner.

PREVENTION

Your most important tool in the control of medical costs is a good prevention program. It's true for human beings and it's equally true for horses. Proper prevention will cost you a little money, but every problem you can't prevent will cost you much more.

Worming

After feeding and watering, worming is the most valuable single service you can provide for your horse. Worms infest every horse's environment. A good manure disposal program can help limit them, but the most sanitary barn and paddock in the world will still be crawling with eggs, worms, and every stage in between. They will inevitably get inside the horse, where they can cause loss of condition, coat problems, and colic. Parasites don't cause every single case of colic, which is the primary killer of adult horses, but they cause so many that parasite control should be a primary goal of every horse owner.

You must worm at least every three months; a two-month schedule is better. Every horse in the barn should be wormed on the same schedule so you don't have parasites in various stages of life, ready to reinfect a recently wormed animal. This makes financial as well as medical sense. You can buy wormers at bulk rates of 5 percent to 10 percent off regular price.

You no longer need a vet or a highly experienced horseman to worm. In the past, the only effective medications had to be introduced in liquid form through a stomach tube, but the same wormers are now available in paste form in single-dose oral syringes. They are not exactly easy to administer,

Worming is one medical procedure that most horse owners can provide for their own animals, if they have help handling the reluctant patient.

but, with the help of a friend and close attention to the directions on the package, you should be able to worm you own horse. Just make sure the entire contents of the tube get inside the horse.

Choosing the medication is a little more complicated. There are many different ones available, mostly because there are many different horse worms to be eradicated. Although the introduction of the broad-spectrum wormer ivermectin has many people using only that medication, many vets still recommend rotating preparations to avoid the development of resistant worms. Ask your vet to recommend a program, buy a recent horse health book, and inquire of experienced horse people what they do for worming. Horse magazines will also help keep you up to date on any new wormers that are introduced.

Don't make your decision on a worming medication based strictly on its price, because none of the paste wormers are expensive. Ivermectin is the most expensive of the pastes, running about $10 per dose at discount, compared to $4 to $6 for the others. But even ivermectin works out to only $5 a month, and that is a bargain by anybody's standards.

Vaccinations

Vaccination is another important part of equine preventive medicine, but you won't have to worry about it as often as worming. Most horses require vaccinations only once a year. You will have to spend a little time deciding which vaccines to give your horse and which, if any, you feel brave enough to administer yourself.

The ideal vaccination program varies from state to state, depending on what contagious diseases are present. You can get the recommended program from a Cooperative Extension office, the state vet's office, or a local veterinarian. But horses everywhere need certain vaccines.

Tetanus is at the top of the list, since horses are particularly susceptible to this often fatal disease. Immunity probably lasts more than a year, but the vaccine is cheap and all experts recommend a yearly booster. Encephalomyelitis doesn't occur everywhere every year, but it pops up often enough that your horse should be vaccinated against whichever of the three strains are possible in your area. The eastern form is almost always fatal to horses, and the Venezuelan form can be transmitted from horses to humans.

A few years ago, rabies vaccination was necessary only for horses in certain parts of North America. But a new epidemic has made the vaccine vital for horses everywhere. The disease is extremely rare in horses, but the fact that it is always fatal and can be transmitted to humans means every domestic animal for which rabies vaccine is approved should be given it every year.

Influenza and rhinopneumonitis vaccines are especially important to horses in contact with other horses. While the diseases are treatable, the vaccines cost a lot less than treatment and most horses are given them each spring. Vaccines for diseases like botulism, strangles, and Potomac Horse Fever are available, but these are usually suggested by veterinarians for use in horses in specific areas.

Should you give vaccinations yourself to save money? Many horse people do. They can save a lot of money doing it, since a clinic visit will cost $20 to $25, a farm call will cost $25 to $35, and each vaccination will cost $10 to $20 (most necessary vaccines are included in a single shot, so don't worry too much about the vaccine total). Instead of paying a vet somewhere between $30 and $50 to vaccinate a horse, you can do the same thing for $6 if you buy a five-way vaccine and syringe through a veterinary supply catalog.

But you have to know what you're doing. Most vets, particularly those who specialize in large animals, are willing to teach you how to give injections. Those whose practices include livestock tend to be especially willing, since they don't expect a farmer to call them to vaccinate a herd of 100 cattle.

The most sensible approach for a horse owner who intends to vaccinate his own animal is to pay for a farm visit or clinic call for an initial vaccination, ask for a recommended schedule for subsequent years, and learn how to do it. Question the vet about possible reactions and other problems.

Many horse owners compromise by paying the vet to do all the primary vaccinations in the spring, then doing any necessary boosters themselves.

In some states, you won't have any choice but to pay a vet to vaccinate. Rabies vaccine can't be shipped to a number of states, so, unless you can find a local source, you will have to have the vet supply the vaccine. If you have an extremely good relationship with your vet, you may be able to buy it from him. Otherwise, you will need a vet visit, because rabies is one vaccine you can't skip. Have him do the other vaccinations while he's there, unless his charge for a five-way vaccine is exorbitant.

A couple of states require prescriptions for needles and vaccines. Your vet might supply these, or you may have to ask him to do the vaccination. Owners who board their horses can often save on veterinarian-administered vaccinations by taking part in a yearly barn clinic. The cost of the farm call is split among the owners, who then pay their own vaccine charges. This can work out to less than $25 a horse, if half a dozen horses are vaccinated. If you take part in a clinic, you probably won't get much opportunity to question the vet about vaccines and procedures, but you will get professional work for less than half the normal price.

Dental Care

Most horses need regular dental care so they can properly utilize their food. Their teeth grow irregularly, and they require rasping, or floating, as often as every six months. Many can get by with a once-a-year appointment.

Large-animal vets will usually float teeth as part of a farm or office visit. Typically, they will add a $25 fee for the service. You can call a specialist in equine dentistry (check ads in horse magazines or ask a friend for a recommendation) but these people will usually charge more, sometimes as much as $50 for a quick routine treatment.

Some people do learn to float their own horse's teeth. The actual procedure of rasping isn't difficult, but getting the horse to behave while you do it can be quite a challenge. You might be able to pay a dentist to teach you how, particularly if you plan to pay him once a year for a primary visit and do a six-month smoothing yourself. You can buy a dental float with separate heads for top and bottom teeth for $30, or one with a sturdy hinged head for $45 from a veterinary supply catalog.

WHEN PREVENTION ISN'T ENOUGH

You can't prevent all illness and injury, so your affordable health care program must include a plan to deal with any problems that develop. You must have a relationship with a veterinarian before something happens. This usually requires paying for at least one visit, at which you have any necessary procedures done. During the visit, ask for all the advice you can get. Your horse will then become a patient of that vet, and you may call in case of emergencies or with questions.

Choosing a Vet
First, locate a list of prospects. You want a vet who does large animal work, of course. A 1991 survey by the American Veterinary Medical Association showed that nearly 30,000 of the more than 50,000 active vets in the United States claim to do equine work. But not all of those 30,000 have equine patients. In fact, only about 1,600 work exclusively with horses, and a few thousand more work exclusively with large animals.

Others have practices equally divided between large and small animals. Even though all vets do some equine work in school, many small-animal specialists haven't touched a horse since graduating. Don't pick a small-animal vet that you talk into dropping by to see your horse. He won't be any cheaper unless he's related to you, and he probably won't be up to date on medications and treatments. You want one who has regular large-animal patients, although you don't need an equine specialist unless your horse has unusual health or lameness problems.

Compile a list of large-animal prospects. With any luck, you'll have several. Eliminate those so far away that they won't be able to see your horse in an emergency. Ask horse owners you respect what they think of the other vets. You are likely to get conflicting opinions on the quality of the vets, depending on who cured whose horse, but you should get a pretty good idea of their reliability in keeping appointments, answering emergency calls, and willingness to allow owners to take over some treatments.

The vet's policy on appointments—whether he does farm visits or office calls for non-emergency work—can determine your choice. Many vets do either, but they usually charge more for the farm visit. If you do not have easy access to a trailer, don't pick a vet who does farm visits only for emergency cases.

If you still have more than one name on the list, check prices. While price shouldn't be the determining factor, it can be used to make a choice between two vets who seem otherwise equal. Most veterinary office receptionists will give you standard fees for procedures over the telephone. Don't be surprised if all the prices in your area are pretty much the same for the same services.

When to Call the Vet

Medical care won't be affordable if you call the vet for every-thing that happens to your horse. But your horse won't be properly cared for if you don't call when he develops something you can't handle yourself. The secret is to know the difference between owner-treatable problems and those that need professional attention. You learn that by self-education. Here's what you should do:

• Subscribe to one good horse magazine. There are dozens, and most include regular health care articles. Talk your barn friends into subscribing to different ones, then share among you.

• Watch every vet call on every horse in the barn. See what the

Subscribing to horse magazines will keep you up to date on new horse health procedures, products, and treatments.

illnesses and injuries look like, and listen closely to the treatment advice. If you feel like you are intruding, volunteer to help hold the horse so the owner can be free to watch the vet work.

- Take owners' short courses at veterinary schools and colleges that offer equine studies. These one- or two-day courses can teach you how to float teeth, how to diagnose colic, even how to trim hooves, sometimes for as little as $10, although most cost more. You'll find them advertised in horse publications.

- Buy at least one good horse health book. Here are some suggestions.

    A-Z of Horse Diseases and Health Problems by Tim Hawcroft (Howell Book House, 1991)

    Horse Owner's Vet Book by Ed Straiton (Lippincott, 1979)

    Horse Owner's Veterinary Handbook by James Giffen and Tom Gore (Howell Book House, 1989)

    How To Be Your Own Veterinarian (Sometimes) by Ruth James (Alpine Press)

Learn What's Normal for Your Horse

You also need to do a complete examination of your healthy horse, so you will have something to compare when he doesn't seem quite right. Record his pulse, respiration, temperature, estimated body weight, and the size and appearance of his normal droppings. Take the pulse by feeling with your fingers—not your thumb—inside the elbow, just above the fetlock, or under the jaw. The average horse has a resting pulse of forty beats a minute. If it's much higher, and the increase can't be explained by recent exercise, the horse may be suffering severe stress.

Respiration is easy to check; just watch the flanks. It should be about twelve to fifteen breaths a minute. If the breathing is much more rapid, or if it becomes noisy, the horse needs close watching. Temperature should be taken with a sturdy veterinary thermometer with a ring to attach a string. This will cost you $4 to $5. You can take a perfectly good horse temperature with a $1.99 human thermometer, but you take the risk of losing the thermometer inside the horse. Normal is 100 to 101 degrees Fahrenheit, a little higher for mares and for all horses in the afternoon. When it reaches 104, the horse has a fever and you usually need to call the vet.

Once you are experienced in home horse health care, you may decide to treat your own horses with antibiotics for fevers and infections. You can buy penicillin through veterinary supply houses without a prescription, and ten days' supply will cost only about $6. Just remember that the problem may be something that a common antibiotic won't handle, or that there may be something newer and more appropriate available.

Since colic is so common and so dangerous, you're going to have to get an idea of what your horse's normal droppings look like. A change in size, consistency, or frequency may indicate a developing digestive problem.

Body weight is important but difficult to determine unless you have access to a livestock scale. But your concern is changes in body weight, not the actual poundage, so absolute accuracy isn't necessary. Many illnesses show up first as a weight loss. You can buy livestock weight tapes for about

$3, but these are often highly inaccurate in terms of both actual weight and changes. The simplest ones give you a scale based entirely on girth measurement, and they sometimes will claim that an 11-hand big-barreled Shetland pony weighs 1,000 pounds. Some tapes ask you to measure body length and girth, and these are somewhat more accurate.

Here's a reasonably accurate formula you can use with a regular tape measure (use one that hasn't stretched). Measure girth, being careful that the horse hasn't swelled his belly thinking that you're about to saddle him. Then measure his length from the high point of the shoulder to the high point of the buttocks. Multiply the girth size in inches by the same figure. Take that total, then multiply it by the body length in inches. That figure should be divided by 330. So a horse with an 80-inch girth measurement and a 70-inch length works out like this: 80 times 80 equals 6,400. 6,400 times 70 equals 448,000. Divide that by 330, and you get a 1,358-pound horse.

Check your horse's vital signs and weight every couple of weeks to keep track of any changes that might signal trouble. If the changes persist, or if they are dramatic, call the vet.

Injuries

You must treat immediately every injury that involves broken skin. That means checking your horse regularly for cuts, nicks, scratches, and abrasions. Minor wounds need only cleaning, but they definitely need that, even if they don't look serious. Others need more serious attention. With experience, you will learn which you can treat and which you need the vet for. In general, these injuries will require veterinary attention:

- any injury with profuse bleeding

- any puncture of a joint, foot, or lower leg

- a fracture

- major damage to support ligaments or tendons

- a high temperature indicating a systemic infection

Most other injuries you can try treating yourself, but if you have any doubts whatsoever, call the vet.

Equip yourself with first aid materials suitable to equine use. Buy a 10 percent solution of povidone iodine, either through a veterinary supply company or at the drugstore. This will cost you about $6 a quart, and you'll be able to use it on almost everything that can infect a horse through his skin, including bacteria, fungi, and some viruses. Use it as an antiseptic wash in solution with plenty of water, or apply it with less water directly to injuries. You can buy it in spray form, but it will cost much more and you'll find yourself dabbing and spreading anyway.

A triple antibiotic ointment will help keep minor injuries from infecting, and wound powder is useful in stopping bleeding and preventing infection. Call for some of the veterinary supply catalogs and take a look at what's available, then ask a vet or an experienced horse person what you should have on hand. These catalogs are also the best sources of affordable wormers, vaccines, medical equipment, and other supplies you need for horse health care. Here are a few good ones:

THE AFFORDABLE HORSE

American Livestock Supply
P.O. Box 8441
Madison, WI 53708-8441
(800) 356-0700

Big D's Tack and Vet Supply
P.O. Box 247
Northfield, OH 44067
(800) 321-2142

Horse Health USA
P.O. Box 9101
Canton, OH 44711-9101
(800) 321-0235

KV Vet Supply
P.O. Box 245
David City, NE 68632
(402) 367-6047

United Vet Equine
14101 West 62nd Street
Eden Prairie, MN 55346
(800) 328-6652

Valley Vet Supply
P.O. Box 504
Marysville, KS 66508-0504
(800) 356-1005

Wiese Vet Supply
P.O. Box 192
Eldon, MO 65026
(800) 869-4373

CHAPTER

TEN

Shoeing

Nature designed the horse's hoof perfectly for his life in the wild. The hoof wall is sturdy, but not so sturdy that it doesn't renew itself by trimming down on the occasional rocky or hard surface the horse encounters during its travels to find fodder. The wall absorbs moisture from grass and mud to remain pliant. The frog cushions the foot as the horse moves forward, the bars balance the pressure from body weight, and the shape of the underside of the foot turns it into a suction cup for safety on wet or smooth surfaces. The entire foot is strong enough to carry the body of the horse without damage to itself.

But as soon as humans start to use the horse, the hoof often becomes inadequate. Instead of the occasional trot across packed dirt, the horse is required to gallop on hard racetracks, jump in arenas that feature an inch or two of soft sand over a much firmer subsurface, or simply walk miles down a paved road. Add to that the fact that the horse now has to carry at least 15 percent more weight in the form of a rider, or pull more than half again his body weight in a carriage, and you have a hoof that wears down far too rapidly. If all that weren't enough, horse fanciers often breed for an animal with a sturdy skeleton and heavy muscles on top of attractive but far too small hooves.

Most ridden or driven horses are shod, and shoeing becomes one of the major ongoing expenses of horse ownership. But you can save money on shoeing without endangering the hoof health of the horse. Here's how.

CHOOSE WELL

Horse buyers pay far too little attention to the hooves of the prospects they examine. You may have no choice with a giveaway or extremely low-priced horse, but any time you are deciding between two or more similar animals, put the quality of their hooves very near the top of your list of pros and cons. This is important not just to save money on shoeing but to acquire a sound, useful horse.

The absence of active hoof injury or illness doesn't qualify a horse as having good hooves. Even a seemingly sound horse with thin, brittle hooves is going to cost you money in shoeing and hoof care. Some equine experts try to avoid horses with white hooves, but others believe that white walls are not necessarily softer than others. Look at the quality of the hoof itself, not just the color. I have a horse with three black and one white hoof. While all four are healthy, the white one is best of all, never suffering from cracks, chips, or anything else.

You want a hoof with thick, uncracked walls, firm surface,

and a concave undersole. The frog should be flexible and not too small. A horse who's been poorly shod or trimmed may have terrible looking hooves that will grow out healthy with good care. Spend some time before selecting a horse examining the hooves of a lot of animals, especially those whose owners have to pay for corrective shoeing. See what to avoid.

GOING BAREFOOT?

Most active horses are going to need some kind of shoeing, and all horses, active or not, are going to need trimming. But far more horses can go barefoot than actually do. If yours is one who can, you can save money and have a very healthy-footed horse at the same time. If he is not a suitable prospect, you can injure him by using him unshod. You have to analyze your horse and his activities before you make the decision.

The Horse
Only a horse with a good, sturdy foot and an even gait should be used unshod. The horn has to be firm enough to take pressure but moist enough not to chip excessively from contact with the ground. The foot has to be well balanced, so that his and your weight are evenly distributed on all surfaces that touch the ground. The foot should also possess a frog that touches the ground, but just barely, and underside walls that form a small bowl. A flatfooted horse is too likely to suffer sole bruises and other injuries to work without shoes.

An examination of a set of shoes pulled from the horse will give you an idea of balance, and a good farrier or a vet will be able to tell from both shoe and hoof whether the

Wear patterns on a shoe can help tell you if a horse is a good candidate for working unshod.

horse has the kind of weight balance in the hooves necessary for barefoot work. Remember that some professionals think every horse should be shod, but a growing number believe that the most natural form of hoof care is best for the health of the animal.

Since even the barefoot horse has to be trimmed every couple of months to even out wear, you can make an appointment with a farrier to do the trim, and then ask his advice on barefoot use during that call. Or ask the vet during his vaccination visit.

The Intended Use

Even a horse with a perfect foot shouldn't go barefoot if he is going to spend a lot of time on hard surfaces, or on any kind of surface if he's going to put in long hours under a heavy rider. A horse pastured in a rocky field may also need the protection offered by metal shoes.

But a horse used lightly in a ring with deep sand, or one who's mostly walked on a grassy trail for an hour or so a day, may do very well barefoot. Shoes pulled from a horse will tell you how much wear he gives his feet. Heavy wear on shoes that were new six weeks ago indicates a poor prospect for going unshod. When one horse of mine could have had her shoes reset a third time, I realized that she was the ideal prospect for barefoot life.

Remember that you can have your horse go barefoot or shod according to the season or changes in your riding activities. Many owners pull shoes in the winter when they don't use their horses regularly. Others find the horses need protection from frozen fields and think shoes add extra traction on ice, but they pull shoes for the summer's leisurely rides on soft woodland trails.

The Advantages of Going Barefoot

Provided his use doesn't cause excessive wear to the horn, the barefoot horse can have a healthier hoof than the shod one. He won't get infections because of nail pricks or scratches from loose clenches. Manure won't pack into his hoof, and he will be less subject to thrush and canker as a result.

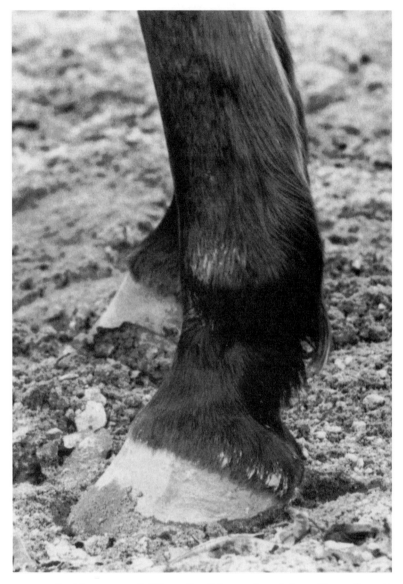

An unshod horse gets full benefit of the moisturizing effects of mud.

SHOEING

While a marshy paddock might lead to too-soft hooves in all horses, shod or unshod, a normal paddock will provide advantages to unshod horses that those with shoes miss out on. Moisture from morning grass and mud is absorbed directly into the wall of the hoof. Since the mud is rarely retained in the hoof, it provides its services without much extra work for you.

Care of the Bare Foot

The fact that your horse isn't shod doesn't mean he needs no care. He should be trimmed, although he probably won't need it quite as often as as a shod animal since he is in no danger of corns, contracted heels, or other hoof problems caused by delaying the trimming of a shod horse.

How often he needs to be trimmed depends on the growth rate of the horn and the wear pattern of the toes. Figure on once every eight weeks, but if the hoof is wearing unevenly, you may have to call the farrier sooner.

Most farriers charge about one-third of their regular rate for trimming and normal shoeing if you want trimming alone. So if your farrier charges $75 for shoeing with new shoes, figure $25 for the trimming.

THE PARTIALLY SHOD HORSE

Many horses who don't quite qualify for going barefoot will do very well with partial shoeing, which usually means shoes on the front feet alone. Again, take a look at an old set of shoes. You may find almost all the wear on the shoes that were removed from the front feet with almost no wear behind.

A farrier can apply full shoes in front, or just grass tips, which are small steel toe shoes often used on breeding stock and retired horses. Active animals may also benefit from grass tips. If they are otherwise qualify for barefoot use but tend to chip a little too much in front, ask your farrier or vet about the advisability of using grass tips.

Partial shoeing won't save you much money, since standard steel keg shoes cost only $5 or $6 each. But the farrier is likely to reduce his labor charge a little, since he has to fit shoes to only two hooves rather than four.

THE SHOD HORSE

Many horses, because of use or conformation, will wear shoes. Such horses in normal riding use are going to have to be trimmed and shod as often as every five weeks, more likely every six or seven weeks, and no longer than every eight weeks. You will not have to shoe so much in winter because hoof growth is slower in cold weather. Older horses may need trimming a little less often, because hoof growth also slows with age. The amount of use the horse gets doesn't matter, unless it's so much that the shoes wear out. It's the trimming that matters.

You can't reduce the cost of shoeing by lengthening the time between visits unless you want to risk the soundness of the horse. But there are a few things you can do.

Choice of Farrier
Picking a farrier according to price is risky, since you might get a cheap bad one who harms your horse's hooves. But it's also wrong to assume that the most expensive is the best. Ask horse-owning friends for recommendations, ask them about price and promptness, and ask about the attitude of

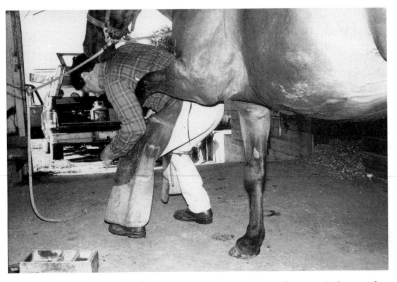

A shod horse will need to see the farrier every five to eight weeks.

the farrier. One who wants to do elaborate corrective shoeing on a basically sound, lightly used pleasure horse may prove too expensive for someone who doesn't have unlimited funds. But one who is so quick and cheap that he overtrims a hoof to make it fit a standard-sized shoe should be avoided at all costs.

The price you pay depends on where you live and the competition among farriers in the area. The price for trimming and shoeing a normal hoof can run from $50 to more than $100 for essentially the same work. Most likely, you will pay between $70 and $80 for trimming and setting new standard shoes, and between $50 and $60 for a trim and reset of the shoes the horse was already wearing. Many farriers will negotiate, especially if you ask them to come to do more than one horse. But even if you have just one horse, ask if there's any way you can get a lower price, perhaps by scheduling an appointment on short notice or something similar.

The fee for shoeing an entire barn may be substantially lower, since the farrier will be able to get a day's work in with just one round trip from his home. Ask your friends about scheduling shoeing clinics.

Hoof Care

You should do everything you can to avoid problems that you'll have to pay to repair. Make sure your horse's hooves get plenty of moisture. They may need dressing or packing, and your veterinary supply catalogs (see Chapter 9) will have plenty of possibilities.

Check regularly for too much growth. A too-early shoeing appointment will cost less in the long run than treatment and corrective shoeing for improper growth.

DO-IT-YOURSELF TRIMMING AND SHOEING

Shoeing is difficult to do and even more difficult to do well, but many owners have learned to shoe their own horses. Many more have learned to trim. It's a possibility to consider if you expect to have a long career of horse ownership.

Horseshoeing schools advertise in horse magazines. Call for their brochures. Most offer two-, four-, and eight-week courses. Even the two-week course will teach you enough to trim your own horses. The eight-week course will not make you a professional blacksmith, but it—as well as the four-week course—will probably teach you enough to do adequate cold shoeing on your own horses.

The two-week courses cost a couple hundred dollars, but

you can make that up by trimming your own horse for two years. Colleges with equine science departments sometimes offer short courses in trimming and shoeing that may be taken by people not enrolled in the program. Call and ask.

You can buy hoof nippers for $12 and a rasp for $8. Even a top quality professional set of trimming tools should cost less than $100. Shoeing equipment will cost you more, but you will be able to buy everything you need for cold shoeing for $250.

Owners not quite ready to get into trimming and shoeing can still learn enough to avoid emergency farrier visits. During your next appointment, ask your farrier how to pull a loose shoe, tighten a loose nail, and pound a protruding clench.

Feeding and Bedding

Horse owners probably waste more money on feed than on any other single aspect of horse care. Encouraged by advertisements and their own consciences, people give their horses a level of nutrition that's not only unneeded, but occasionally harmful. Good nutrition can actually be cheaper than poor nutrition.

Still, any effort to save money on feed should be done with care, since feeding errors can lead to health problems. Horses adjust poorly to sudden changes in feed, whether it's a new kind of grain, turnout in a new, rich pasture, or a substantial change in the ratio of concentrated feed to forage. Before you establish an affordable feeding program or make changes in an existing program, learn something about equine nutrition.

FEED REQUIREMENTS

A good horse health book or general book on horsekeeping
will give you information on the nutritional requirements of
horses. Your County Extension office or the office of the
horse specialist in your state's Department of Agriculture
may have free booklets with the same information.

In simple terms, here's what you will find. The average
horse needs 2 percent of its total body weight each day in
feed. So a 1,000-pound horse requires 20 pounds per day of
feed, which can be divided up among pasture, hay, and grain
or commercial horse feed. Individual animals may need more
or less than this, depending on whether they gain or lose
weight on the 2 percent figure.

Obviously, the cheapest way to feed a horse is to have him
obtain all his requirements from grazing. In some cases, this
can work. An unworked small horse grazing on good, growing grass may get sufficient calories and enough food volume
to thrive on pasture alone. Most pleasure horses will need
something more, but many of them will need only additional
hay if they are not heavily worked.

At less than 10 cents a pound even when bought by the
single bale, hay is a nutritional bargain for horses. It can
provide everything almost any horse needs, provided it is of
good quality. Alfalfa hay is richest of all hays in terms of
protein and nutrients, but it may actually provide too much
protein and calcium for all but growing horses. Grass hay,
which costs about 50 cents a bale less than alfalfa in most
areas, is often a better all-around choice for pleasure horses,
although the excess nutrients in alfalfa can be balanced out
with enough grazing.

Hay should form the base of any affordable feeding pro-

Good pasture can make up a significant percentage of a horse's diet, but most pleasure horses will need supplementary hay or grain.

gram. You will need to add grain or commercial feed if your horse can't maintain his weight on hay alone, if you can't buy top-quality leafy hay, or if your horse works so hard he can't get enough calories from hay.

Most owners feed at least some grain to their pleasure horses, ranging from perhaps a 70–30 hay to grain ratio for horses who work an hour or so a day to a 50–50 division for horses who work more. The hay percentage shouldn't drop below 50 except for horses who can't manage hay due to dust allergies. Most horses need at least 50 percent of their diets in the form of hay or pasture to keep their stomachs full and themselves busy.

Saving on Grain

Grain or horse feed is more expensive than hay. There are two approaches to saving money on the grain your horse needs. One is to buy pure grains from the feed store according to what is available and reasonable, then mix and match to provide optimum calories and nutrients. If you have any interest in doing this, you will have to know more about nutrition than if you rely on commercial mixes.

The most important source of information on equine nutrition is the National Academy of Science's *Nutrient Requirements of Horses*. Write the National Academy Press, 2101 Constitution Avenue N.W., Washington, DC for purchase information. This book provides nutritional analyses of various grains and offers charts of the requirements of horses according to age, size, and activity.

You must avoid making sudden changes if you use a variety of grains. Any changeover from one grain to another should be gradual, with one phased out while another is phased in. You can save money by buying pure grains. Digestible crimped oats will probably be about 3 cents a pound cheaper than a middle-range complete feed, while whole oats may be as much as 4 cents a pound cheaper. Bran will be cheaper still. But you may find you need several different grains and a lot of storage space to provide the nutrients your horse requires. You will definitely have to allot more time to feeding than if you pick a prepared feed.

For most owners, buying brand-name commercial feed is the most sensible, the safest, and sometimes even the most economical approach to providing grain to a horse. You save money by buying the cheapest label offered by the company you choose. Unless your horse is a mare in the last three months of her pregnancy, a nursing mother, or an animal younger than two, he will get everything he needs in the lowest-priced feed of the dozen or so offered by the feed producer.

In commercial horse feeds, price is based primarily on protein content of the feeds. At my local feed store, which charges typical prices for the brand it carries, a 10 percent protein sweet feed costs $6.20 for a 50-pound bag. A 16 percent sweet feed costs $7.15. Most of those 16 percent bags go out the door with the owners of adult pleasure horses.

According to the National Research Council, a mature horse needs only 8 to 9 percent protein in his diet, regardless of how much work he does. Some draft breeds in hard use require about 10 percent, and mares of any breed in late pregnancy and during lactation need 10 to 12 percent.

The only horses that really need that 16 percent are pre-weaned foals during their creep feeding period. Owners of well-loved horses apparently think that the high protein feed will help their animals perform and feel better, particularly if those horses work hard. But the heavily used horses may just need more calories in their feed. That means more feed, not higher-protein feed.

There is no clear link between excess protein and disease in adult horses, although some scientists suspect that too much protein may be as hard on the kidneys in horses as it is in human beings. Some studies have suggested that excess protein fed to growing horses can actually slow down growth. A little too much protein probably does more damage to your bank account than to your horse, but there is no point in paying for something that does no good and may actually do some harm. If you just can't bring yourself to give 10 percent feed, move up to the 12 percent. Stay away from the 16 percent, even if the feed bag has a shiny racehorse or Grand Prix jumper on the label. Even they don't need the 16 percent.

The label on the feed bag does have something worthwhile: a recommended feeding schedule, suggesting how much you should give according to your horse's size and the work he does. The label, or a more complete booklet published by the feed company, will suggest hay–grain combinations that should work well for your horse's circumstances.

Avoid Overfeeding

Don't equate the fat horse with the healthy one. A horse whose ribs you can't feel without pressing down firmly is too fat, and his weight will put extra pressure on his limbs, joints, and feet. While too much fat doesn't seem to be related to heart disease and cancer in horses quite as much as it is in humans, excess weight is clearly related to unsoundness. You do your horse no good by making him plump and you spend extra money doing it.

Other Money-Saving Tips

There are several additional things you can do to help save on the feed bill.

- Buy in quantity whenever you can because the price per bag will usually be lower. But you will need dry and secure storage space that neither rodents nor loose horses can reach. Once you get the feed home, either remove it from the bags or put it, bag

Feed bins with heavy lids in a dry, secure room will permit you to buy grain in bulk.

and all, into feed bins with heavy lids. If you don't have feed bins and don't want to build them, you can use big garbage cans with tight-fitting lids.

- Watch the weather when you buy in quantity. Commercial pellets should stay fresh for several weeks regardless of the weather, but you may have problems with sweet feeds during very hot or very cold weather. The molasses that holds these feeds together may become moldy in hot and humid weather and may freeze when the temperature drops. Frozen feed is annoying, but moldy feed can be deadly. Buy only the quantity

A coffee can makes an adequate grain scoop, but weigh the amount you get in each can so you don't over- or underfeed.

you can use up within a week or so during periods of extreme temperatures.

- Don't guess on the amount you distribute at each feeding. Empty coffee cans make perfectly good feed scoops, but weigh one full can with each kind of feed you use so you know exactly how much you are scooping into each feed bucket. One can each of pure grains, pelleted feed, sweet feed, and extruded feed will show four different weights.

- While you shouldn't store feed in the bag it comes in, don't throw the bags away. The plastic ones will make the best garbage bags you've ever used, while the burlap ones make excellent rags, good dry storage for kindling, and perfect shepherds' costumes for Nativity pageants. Even the paper bags can be used for composted horse manure before you give it to your neighbors or sell it to gardeners.

SUPPLEMENTS

Horses rarely need nutritional supplements if they are being fed a brand-name commercial feed. Buy a supplement only if your vet diagnoses a specific deficiency. Otherwise, you may be wasting money and may even be endangering the horse. Vitamins A and D, for example, are stored in the body and a well-fed horse can get toxic levels if he is oversupplemented with these and certain other nutrients.

Horses whose diets consist primarily of good-quality pasture or hay usually get all the nutrients they need too. If you have doubts about the quality of the forage, a simple, low-priced vitamin supplement might be a good idea. You don't need megadose vitamins, just a supplement that provides no more than 100 percent of the horse's daily requirements.

Supplements are available in feed and tack stores, but you will find the lowest prices through discount supply catalogs (see Chapter 12). Identify the best buy by figuring the per-day cost of the recommended dosage, not by the price of the package.

Although relatively few horses really need commercial supplements, every horse should have access to salt. Adding loose salt to feed is the cheapest way to provide it, but salt blocks are easier on the owner and not much more expensive.

The best deal of all is the combined salt and trace mineral block, the one that's red rather than white. Since horses virtually never overdose themselves on salt, you don't have to worry about them taking in too much of a particular mineral. Order a $3 bracket from a supply catalog, then buy a $1 salt-mineral block from the feed store. It's best to buy the block locally, since stores in areas where certain nutrients are lacking in soil (selenium, for example) will stock blocks that contain those nutrients. The block will last for months and the bracket will last for years.

WATER

All horses need free access to clean, fresh drinking water at all times. A horse of average size will drink six to twelve gallons of water a day at rest, more during summer and during periods of heavy exercise. A pond or stream can provide low-cost turnout water, although you may have to keep it clear of ice during the winter. A tub within reach of a hose can substitute for natural water.

A $1 salt-mineral block is the cheapest and best food supplement you can buy.

The horse will also need water indoors. The cheapest way to provide it is to buy a good-quality polyethylene twenty-quart bucket ($7 to $13) and carry water to the stall. You will have to do this one to three times a day, depending on how much time the horse spends indoors. There are various other systems that make watering easier, including individual faucets in each stall, automatic waterers, and water tank heaters. They are more expensive than hauling, but you may find the investment worthwhile because of the time it saves you.

BEDDING

Stabled horses require bedding, and some owners like to provide bedding in outdoor sheds for field-kept animals. Bedding enables horses to sleep comfortably and allows waste materials to drain from the surface, keeping the horse clean and dry. How much you need depends on how much time the horse spends indoors.

The average horse urinates and defecates six to eight times a day, and if he does most of that in his stall you may need one or more bales a day of new bedding. If he spends only the night indoors, you may need only a couple of fresh bales a week.

There are several different bedding materials, each of which has pros and cons. Straw is light, absorbent, easily stored, but tends to cause dry hooves and is sometimes eaten by horses. Pine shavings are absorbent and light, but they require a lot of storage space. Horses like the feel of sawdust, but it is—understandably—dusty. Peat moss has superb compost value but is usually expensive and hard to find, at least in the United States.

FEEDING AND BEDDING

Strictly in terms of price, the best value in bedding depends on where you live. In the northern United States and Canada, you will probably find pine shavings to be so much more reasonable than other bedding materials that you won't consider anything else. In my area, a single bale of shavings at the feed store costs about $3.80, while a similar-sized bale of straw is $5.50. In the South, you may find straw to be the cheaper material. In sugarcane-producing areas, shredded and dried cane may be available at a low price, in peanut-producing areas you'll find peanut hulls, and in newsprint-producing areas you may find shredded newspaper.

Regardless of which product you settle upon as your affordable bedding material, here are some guidelines to help you save money.

- Buy as much as you can safely store, because the per-bale price will be dramatically lower for bulk purchases than for single bales. My $4 bale of pine shavings costs $2 a bale if I can buy a truckload from a lumbermill, or $3 a bale if I buy a hundred bales from the feed store. Your bedding storage place doesn't have to be quite as dry or nearly as rodent-proof as your feed storage, but it shouldn't be damp. If you can't store a truckload, try to work out a deal with your horse-owning neighbors in which you split up a big shipment.

- Extend the time your horse spends outdoors. For every three hours the horse spends in a field, there will be two less damp or soiled sections of bedding to be removed and discarded.

- If prices are otherwise similar, choose a bedding material that composts most easily to spread on your own property or to sell as manure. Peat moss tops the list, although it certainly won't be cheapest to obtain, followed by wheat straw, barley straw, and pine shavings.

- Don't try to save money by delaying stall cleaning. Manure and damp spots have to be removed daily, and the bedding will have to be completely changed when the whole surface seems a little damp. Permitting a horse to stand in damp bedding can lead to hoof disease and infection, which you'll have to pay a vet to treat.

C H A P T E R

T W E L V E

Jack and Equipment

Among the pleasures of horse ownership is acquiring equipment to use while riding and caring for your horse. It's fun to shop for, it's fun to buy, and it's fun to try out. Even if you could get along without equipment, you wouldn't want to. But you don't need to buy as much as you think you do, and you certainly don't need to spend a lot of money on it.

Some items you must have to effectively use and care for a horse. These basics should be of good quality, since you will use them again and again. But even they can be found at bargain prices. First, let's take a look at what you can't get along without.

WHAT YOU REALLY NEED

To handle a horse, you need a sturdy halter and a lead rope. In fact, it's wise to have a few sets around, because you never

A couple of extra halters around the barn help provide low-cost insurance against loose-horse emergencies.

know when a horse might get loose without a halter. While you want your primary halter to be sturdy, you can buy an adequate standby halter and rope for about $7. Have a couple around the place for very cheap insurance.

To ride, you need a bridle to direct and control the horse. Bridles come in a wide price range, but you will find a simple bridle with a plain bit to be the best buy at all price levels. It will also be the most suitable bridle for the average pleasure horse and rider.

If you ride English style, pick a plain hunt-style bridle with a large-ringed snaffle bit. Most bridles come with nosebands, but they are unnecessary for most horses that do not use martingales. If you can find a cheaper one without the noseband, it will probably suit your purposes. Remember that you can add a noseband later if you choose to. If you ride western, you can buy a simple one- or two-ear headstall bridle with a plain curb bit.

You will also need a saddle of some kind, and this will prove to be a bigger investment than the bridle. You will find English saddles to be a little cheaper than western saddles of similar quality, but remember that western saddles normally come with fittings, including stirrups and girth. You may have to buy these items separately if you pick an English saddle, and that may make the prices essentially the same. You can find bareback riding pads with simple girth and stirrups for about $25, and an expert rider may find these suitable for very casual riding. But most riders will need a real saddle for security and comfort.

Unless the saddle you pick fits your horse extremely well, is well padded, and is easily cleaned, you will need a saddle pad to prevent chafing and to absorb sweat and dirt. Even if your saddle doesn't seem to require a pad, get one anyway.

A simple bridle, saddle, pad, and girth of respectable quality can be had for less than $150, if you search for discount and used equipment.

A plain one is very cheap protection against damage to your much more expensive horse and saddle.

You will probably need grooming equipment for your horse. Even if he is boarded at a stable that provides equipment, you don't want grooming tools that have been used on other horses to be used on yours. Too many parasites and skin diseases can be spread through brushes and rags. Grooming tools aren't expensive, although you can end up spending a lot of money if you buy everything available, most of which you will never use. You can get by with one soft brush, one firm brush, and a hoof pick. Total cost—about $7. Use rags for preliminary mud removal and polishing, and use paper towels for eye, sheath, and under-tail cleaning.

TACK AND EQUIPMENT

You don't even need horse shampoo. Horses who spend most of their time outdoors need oil and even dust in their coats for protection from cold, heat, sun, and flies. Only caked mud must to be thoroughly removed. If your horse becomes dirtier than you can bear, use a little of your own shampoo to bathe him. It's basically the same stuff.

If you have to provide feed and water buckets, buy some that are designed for livestock use. They are no more expensive—and are often cheaper—than general-purpose buckets of similar size, and they will survive horse assaults much better. Traditionally, horse people have used heavy-duty plastic for feed and water buckets, but many owners now use black rubber, especially for ground feeding tubs. They are harder to clean than plastic, but they withstand the most aggressive horses with little injury to either themselves or the animals. The rubber buckets and tubs used to be more expensive, but prices are now similar to those for plastic.

To clean stalls, you will need a fork suitable to the kind of bedding you use, and you will need something to carry soiled bedding away from the stall. Typically, people buy a manure basket to carry the day's soiled bedding to the wheelbarrow, which is then wheeled to the manure pile. You will probably find it just as easy—and cheaper—to skip the manure bucket and just use the wheelbarrow.

That's it for the absolute necessities. Your individual horse care circumstances will undoubtedly dictate additional purchases, such as crossties if none are available at your stable, hooks to hang tubs, and so on. You will also buy other things, not so much because you need them but because you want them. Whether your purchases are necessities, luxuries, or something in between, you can save money. Here are the three approaches to affordable buying.

BUYING AT DISCOUNT

The first and most important secret to paying less for new equipment is to stay out of most tack shops except in emergencies and during special sales. If you break a girth in the morning and are competing in a show in the afternoon, you may have no choice. Otherwise, stay away except to check the bulletin board or to take a close look at some new item of equipment. Control yourself, though. Many tack shops charge nearly twice what you pay through mail order. Some try to approach mail-order prices, but overhead makes discounting difficult for them.

Order catalogs from the mail-order tack and equipment supply companies. There is some overlap with veterinary suppliers, and you may find attractively priced equipment in the catalogs you ordered for your horse health supplies. But the best buys will be from the companies that specialize in discount tack. Start with catalogs from these companies. You'll probably receive additional catalogs once you start ordering.

Chick's
P.O. Box 59
Harrington, DE 19952
(800) 444-2441

Dover Saddlery
P.O. Box 5837
Holliston, MA 01746
(800) 989-1500
(Dover is less a discount service
than an extremely well-

Acquire tack catalogs before you shop for new or used horse equipment.

stocked supply house. You'll find what you need in all price ranges here.)

*Libertyville Saddle Shop
P.O. Box M
Libertyville, IL 60048-4913
(800) 872-3353*

*State Line Tack
P.O. Box 1217
Plaistow, NH 03865-1217
(800) 228-9208*

THE AFFORDABLE HORSE

Western International, Inc.
395 Freeport Boulevard, Unit 2
Sparks, NV 89431
(800) 634-6737

Is it worth taking the time to call for the catalogs, then placing an order and waiting a week for delivery? Absolutely. Here are some examples. A plain leather bridle of moderate quality with a raised noseband and laced reins costs $39 at my local tack store. A similar bridle is about $20 through mail order. A metal hoof pick is $1.19 at the tack store, 55 cents in the catalogs. The $200 basic saddle from the tack store goes for $100 in a catalog.

Of course, you can buy $1,000 saddles through mail order, too, but you will get a saddle that might cost twice that at a store. Your selection through mail order will be greater than in even the best-stocked tack store, and most companies will take unused returns (although you will have to pay for return shipping).

How about quality? Are you getting something decent when you buy through mail order? The companies mentioned above (and several other established companies whose catalogs you will begin to receive) are careful about the quality of the equipment they offer. Even the lowest-price items in their selections will be fully usable for pleasure riders.

For most items of horse equipment, buying through discount mail order is the most sensible and reasonable approach. But for certain expensive items, particularly saddles and other leather goods, there is another approach to consider.

BUYING USED EQUIPMENT

It makes little sense to buy used grooming equipment, since new brushes, picks, and combs are available at such reasonable prices through mail order. Used ones are likely to be worn, to need serious cleaning, and to cost about the same as new ones. It makes more sense to look for used saddles, since new saddles tend to be expensive. This is particularly true if you want something better than the basic model.

Fortunately, used saddles of all quality levels are available, since riders buy new saddles at about the same rate that drivers buy new cars. People want better saddles, different saddles, or just new saddles, usually long before their old saddles wear out. How do you find these saddles?

The best source is the tack shop—the place with all those shiny new $500 saddles on display out front. Many tack shops don't advertise the fact that they have a selection of used saddles, since they would much rather sell you a new one. But most of them also take saddles in trade and have a selection available at all times. Call each shop in your area and ask if they carry used equipment. If they do, you will find that the owner is much more willing to negotiate price on used equipment than on new items, so you may be able to talk a good saddle down to a real bargain level.

Some tack shops specialize in used equipment, usually placed by an owner on consignment. The owner gets paid, minus a commission, only if the saddle is sold. Consignment saddles are usually a little more expensive than trade-in saddles, and the shop owner may not be able to negotiate a lower price. But a good-quality consignment saddle will almost always be lower in price than the same saddle new.

You will also find individual used saddles advertised in

local horse publications, and on bulletin boards at stables and feed stores. Before you begin looking at used saddles, open your mail-order catalogs to get an idea of what new saddles at the various levels of quality cost. You don't want to pay a new saddle price for something of a similar quality that has been used, but you may decide that a used top-quality saddle is worth the same to you as a new saddle of lower quality.

Other tack items also show up as used equipment. Bridles, bits, stirrups, and girths are traded in or replaced with better or different models and become available. Again, find out what you would pay for a new version before shopping for a used one.

Before you buy used equipment, decide how much wear the item shows and whether the wear will negatively affect its usability. In saddles, a stretched or torn stirrup leather doesn't matter at all, since you can buy a new pair of leathers for $20. Just make sure that you take that cost into consideration. You can also replace stirrups, girths, and billet straps for minimal cost.

But misshapen padding means that the saddle will have to be restuffed by an expert, and that may cost as much as buying a new basic saddle. A broken tree may be impossible to repair by anybody. Bridles with loose stitching can be easily repaired, but one with a broken strap will probably cost too much to fix to be a good buy. But you will have to use your own judgment on each item of used equipment that you consider.

One piece of equipment that is usually best bought new is a safety helmet for yourself. One accident in which a helmet suffers a hard blow might be enough to render it useless for head protection. You can't always tell by feeling it if the protective shell has been cracked. Unless you know the history of the helmet and trust the original owner to tell you the truth about it, buy a new helmet. You can get a certified safety helmet through mail order for as little as $45.

BUYING NON-TRADITIONAL MATERIALS

A third approach to finding bargains in horse equipment is to choose items made of materials that are lower in cost but not lower in usability. In fact, many less common and cheaper materials are preferable to the more traditional ones.

The least expensive girths are made of mohair or nylon blend strings. They are washable, non-slip, non-chafing, absorbent, and cost as little as $10 through mail order. English style riders often look down on string girths, considering them to be inferior to leather. They shouldn't. Why pay five times as much money for something that doesn't work noticeably better? Western riders have used string cinches for decades without undue loss of either saddles or status.

Nylon halters, which cost about half of what leather halters of equivalent quality do, used to be looked down upon as well. But they are so sturdy and so easy to clean even the most traditional horse people now use them. Some experts warn against leaving a nylon halter on a stabled or turned-out horse, since it won't break and free him if he catches his halter on something.

You can also find a good nylon bridle for much less than the equivalent bridle in leather. Nylon bridles have not proven as popular as nylon halters, but they are equally sturdy and easy to maintain. You may see more of them in the future as more people turn to affordable horsekeeping.

Riders are already turning in increasing numbers to saddles made of synthetic materials. The best known of these saddles are made of a nylon-based fabric produced under the trade name Wintec. They are lighter than leather saddles, they wash and dry easily, they don't stiffen or dry out with age, and they cost the same or less than leather saddles of equivalent quality. You can find them new through mail order ($250 to $300 for an all-purpose saddle) and sometimes used in tack shops for even less.

MAKING YOUR OWN

You can make some items of horse equipment yourself. A saddle pad is easy. An old bed pad or a yard of quilted material from the fabric store can be hemmed into a rectangle or, using an old contoured pad as a pattern, into a pad that fits precisely under an English saddle. You can do the same with fake fleece.

You can easily make your own girth covers, coolers, and anything else that doesn't require specialized equipment. Just make sure you aren't wasting your time on something that you can buy ready-made just as cheaply as you can make it. I recently spent an hour and $8 worth of fabric making a saddle pad just before finding a fully bound quilted pad complete with billet straps in a sales circular for $6.90.

MAKING YOUR EQUIPMENT LAST

The easiest way to save money on equipment is to not have to buy it more often than necessary. If you maintain your equipment with care, it will last longer and you will have to replace it less often. The most important step in maintenance

Maintain your equipment to make it last. Wash what you can, and clean and dry everything else.

is drying everything that gets wet. The second most important step is keeping everything clean.

All leather goods have to be dried off to prevent mildew, which causes leather to deteriorate. If a little mold or mildew has appeared on your tack, wash it with a very small amount of bleach mixed with water. The bleach will kill the mildew. You must then thoroughly dry the leather, then soften it with a leather conditioner. Most metals used in modern tack are rust resistant, but you should keep your metal fittings dry too, just in case.

Non-leather equipment should be washed regularly. This includes nylon halters, saddle pads, cord girths, brushes, hoof picks, and other grooming equipment. Not only will the equipment last longer, you will also help prevent skin diseases from attacking your horse. That saves on vet bills and medications.

C H A P T E R

T H I R T E E N

Insurance

Many people trying to make horse ownership affordable don't even think about insurance. In some cases, they are being perfectly sensible. But in other cases, they are taking needless chances. Do you need insurance for your horse-related activities? Yes and no. First, what you probably don't need.

MORTALITY INSURANCE

Owners of valuable horses almost always insure their animals' lives, but even these owners often don't need to do it. The only horses who really should be insured for mortality are those in whom the owners have invested a great deal of money or those whose earnings or eventual sale price are earmarked for important bills or expenses. The rule of thumb is: if you can afford the financial blow of the loss of the horse, don't pay the money for mortality premiums.

To be fair, mortality insurance isn't particularly expensive when figured as a percentage of the animal's value. Count on an annual premium of 3 to 4 percent of the stated value of the horse, provided he's under the age of about fifteen and is used in non-racing activities. That means that a $1,000 horse will cost $30 to $40 a year to insure. But the company will require a $250 to $500 deductible and may exclude payment for death from any conditions that might have caused him to be worth so little. Many companies require a preinsurance physical for even low-value horses, and this will raise your cost considerably.

Don't try to insure him for more than he's worth, either. If he dies, you will have to prove his real value, either with a sales slip, testimony from experts, or show ring ribbons.

MEDICAL AND SURGICAL INSURANCE

Health insurance might appear to be a better buy for owners of affordable horses, but this is often not the case. This is an evolving field and the facts may eventually change, but medical and surgical insurance is currently a rather poor investment for most owners. The primary problem is that medical insurance is usually available only as a rider to mortality policies, so you can't buy it alone.

The other problem is that you have to pay a large premium for limited coverage. A typical medical policy provides you with $5,000 emergency medical coverage—with no coverage for worming, vaccinations, or other routine care—for $125 to $150 a year. There will be exclusions, primarily for illnesses that the horse has had within a one- or two-year period. There will also be a deductible—probably $250—that you must cover before the insurance begins to pay. For $5,000 of surgical coverage, the premium will be $75 to $150, 'and the deductible will also be smaller. But many of these policies cover only the surgical procedure, not aftercare.

If you love your low-priced horse so much that you know you would pay for major surgery or medical care, you might consider a mortality-medical package. For a $1,000 horse, that would cost you between $230 and $340 per year.

LOSS OF USE

Owners of show horses sometimes buy loss-of-use policies, so that they get some compensation if the horse goes lame or develops an illness that prevents him from doing what he was bought to do. Don't even consider this for a low-priced pleasure horse, even if you can find someone to write a policy for you. It will cost you an annual premium of 2 to 3 percent of the value of the horse, and you may have a hard time collecting on it if something does happen.

LIABILITY INSURANCE

Now, for something you do need. Everybody who owns a horse should make sure that the horse is covered by some kind of liability policy. No matter how careful you are and how sensible your horse is, he could spook, run away, and injure someone. Many regular homeowner's insurance policies include coverage of a horse used by the owner and members of the family for pleasure purposes. Many more umbrella policies, which you buy to add liability coverage to your home or car insurance, will cover non-commercial use of horses.

Check your policies to make sure that horses are not specifically excluded from your policy. If they are, consider changing insurance companies to make sure they are. That will probably be the cheapest way to make sure you are covered for injuries caused by your horse.

If you don't own a home or car and don't have a basic policy, you can buy an equine liability policy just for your own horse. A million-dollar policy for a single pleasure horse shouldn't cost more than $100 to $200 a year, possibly less if nobody uses him except you and your family.

WHEN YOUR HORSE IS LEASED OR LENT

Your homeowner's, umbrella, or equine liability policy may be affected if you lease your horse to somebody else. Check with your agent and request, in writing, a clarification of your coverage according to the circumstances.

If your horse is to be used in a lesson program, your coverage will almost certainly be affected, since his use will become commercial. Ask that you be named as an additional insured person on the stable's policy. It shouldn't cost them anything extra and it will give you protection if a student is injured while aboard your horse.

HOW TO FIND EQUINE INSURANCE

First, talk to your regular insurance agent. He probably won't handle equine mortality or medical policies, but he can clarify if your family policies cover any liability you might incur. You may be well covered already, or you may only have to buy an umbrella policy—at $150 to $200 a year—that will give you a million dollars' worth of additional liability coverage for your home, your car, your horse, and anybody that you might slander.

If you need something more complex, find an agent who specializes in equine insurance. Dozens of them advertise in horse publications, but local recommendations may be better. Ask the manager of the best-run stable or farm in your area to tell you which agency handles their insurance. Also ask if they would recommend that agency. If you like what you hear, call the agency.

Remember that you can shop around for insurance just like you can for anything else. Quotes don't cost anything, so get several. But don't automatically accept the lowest quote. Find out which insurance carrier the agency plans to use for your policy, then make sure that the company is in good financial shape. An agent can provide you with a report on the company (if he's reluctant to show you a ratings report, consider that a red flag). Your state's insurance regulatory commission or your local library can help you find financial health ratings of particular insurance companies.

Read everything in the policy before you pay the premium. Equine insurance policies are known for being filled with exclusions and exceptions. The exclusions may not bother you, but they may eliminate some provision that you specifically want and need.

I N D E X

INDEX

INDEX

INDEX

INDEX

Pocket in front